Save Money and Save The Earth

How Your Business Can Do Both

Kathi A. Haas

Marketing Methods Press
Phoenix, Arizona

Library of Congress Catalog Card Number: 91-051087

ISBN 0-9624798-3-7

Author, Kathi A. Haas

Printed in the United States of America

This book offers information about products and practices used by others that have provided beneficial results for their businesses. We believe the information and ideas provided to us for the book are accurate and, as much as possible, free from bias. We cannot and do not guarantee the same results for your business. This book offers you a start and challenges you to seek ways for your business to save money and save the earth, too. Quantity discounts and special editions of the book are available. Please see the last page for details.

PRINTED ON RECYCLED PAPER.

Dedication

For our children, Kevin and Allison. May they learn to cherish and protect the earth.

Acknowlegements

This book was written to help businesses of all sizes save money and save the earth. The many companies whose case studies are included in the book must be thanked for their willingness to share information on what their companies are doing, for the book would not have been possible without their ready cooperation. It is interesting and encouraging to see that so much is being done. I hope businessmen and businesswomen reading this book will get ideas on what they can do, too.

Special thanks goes to Ann Parker and Heather Hitzeman for their research and information gathering and to Lori Yoney and Niko Lambesis for their assistance during the production stages. The cover was designed by Cindy Mackey.

I also want to thank my parents, Betty and Bill Hostert, and my husband, Richard, for their interest, encouragement and support, and for keeping the kids entertained while I worked on the book. It would not have happened without them.

Table Of Contents

Chapter 1

Saving The Earth Is Good Business

"Much lies ahead to be done. Our intent is to be proactive in carrying out our environmental policy. As individuals and as institutions, we each have a role to play."

Edwin L. Artzt,
Chairman & Chief Executive
The Proctor & Gamble Company

"There's no question that being perceived as environmentally responsible is an asset in today's business environment. But the perception must be based on responsible actions and not on media hype."

Allan H. Doane
Vice President, Corporate Quality Assurance
& Environmental Compliance
Warner-Lambert Company

"Eight of 10 Americans are Environmentalists....,"

Wall Street Journal, August 2, 1991

Today's consumers think of themselves as environmentalists. That's the most important reason why saving the earth is good business. The people who buy your products and services expect you to do your part to preserve and protect the earth and its natural resources for future generations.

Simply providing quality goods and services and adding to the economic growth and prosperity of our country is not enough. Most Americans also expect businesses to carry out their enterprise with little or no disruption to the environment. Our national values have changed and our collective vision has broadened. Today, if you want to attract and retain customers, it makes good business sense to incorporate sound environmental practices in daily business operations.

Will sticking biodegradable or recyclable labels on every product going out the door do the trick? Probably not! While companies who do so might be able to exploit the consumer's newfound interest in environmental protection for a short while, it will be the companies that make a sustained commitment to saving the earth that will enjoy public support in the long run. The public's concern for the environment is here to stay and smart companies will change their business operations to make sure they will keep their customers coming back.

The government also expects business to do its part. That's another reason to take interest in the subject. Many states are enacting strict environmental protection laws. Regulations at the federal, state and local levels are being initiated to deal with hazardous waste, resource conservation, pollution prevention and recycling. Some states are taking a positive approach by providing tax breaks and other incentives for businesses taking specific steps to save the earth. Other states are taking a punitive approach to enforcing environmental protection by charging fines and, in extreme cases, shutting businesses down. Most offer a combination of rewards and punishment to stimulate compliance.

The important thing to remember is that public opinion drives government regulations. If business owners take voluntary action, they can beat the command-and-control approach of government regulators, who are sure to make their lives miserable and increase their stress levels, not to mention stifle their creative approaches to solving environmental problems.

Saving the earth also is good for the bottom line. Many companies have found that instituting selected programs in recycling, waste reduction, pollution control and conservation have lead to substantial dollar savings or have generated additional revenue. Resourceful entrepreneurs have established entire new companies as a result of the environmental movement. They have found ways to recapture, reuse or reconstitute resources that were normally sent to the landfill and have turned them into usable goods. Others have developed new items that meet the public's demand for environmentally safe products and services. Ample evidence that cost savings are possible is documented in the success stories that follow.

Saving the earth can do wonders for a company's public relations image, making people feel good about the business and its products and services. That's another reason why saving the earth is good business. Employees like to work for companies that respect the environment. Existing and potential customers like to spend their dollars with companies that are viewed as environmentally sensitive. Corporate environmentalism can be turned into a competitive advantage, helping to attract quality employees and loyal customers.

Reduce, Reuse, Recycle

Every company no matter how large or small does two things; they consume energy and resources and they produce waste. To make real progress in protecting the environment and conserving our natural resources, experts have offered a simple formula: reduce, reuse and recycle.

While recycling seems to get all the attention and will be addressed at length in the next chapter, it should be the last step in the process. By reducing the amount of unnecessary packaging, the size and number of printed reports, the use of toxins and pollutants, the number of unnecessary trips using the company vehicle, the amount of mail sent, the number of memos generated, the number of copies produced at the copy machine, and the amount of energy to heat, cool and light the facility, a business can have a major impact on resource conversation and enjoy direct savings. A simple directive to "cut back ... make do with less" will not only help save the earth, but could save a business, especially during difficult economic times. By taking steps to reduce what you use, you also will be generating less trash and creating less pollution.

At times, reusing something is better than recycling it. Reusing a product over and over again can save the time and cost of breaking it down to materials that can be remanufactured into something new. Make a habit of purchasing products that can be used over and over again. For example, use refillable pens instead of disposable ones. Buy office furniture and equipment that have been reconditioned. Use coffee mugs instead of throwaway styrofoam cups. Buy in bulk and refill the same "single serving" containers over and over again. Reusing items saves resources and eliminates garbage from the waste stream.

Unfortunately, businessmen and businesswomen have been viewed traditionally as the great destroyers, plunderers and exploiters of the environment and its precious resources. American enterprise takes the blame for most of the world's environmental problems. The truth is, while businesses have contributed to our environmental woes, it's the collective damage caused by careless and irresponsible acts of individuals that has the greatest negative impact on our earth - its land, air and water. For example, more oil is spilled on the earth by careless individuals disposing of used motor oil each year than was spilled in the Alaskan *Valdez* oil cargo ship mishap.

Now that people have realized the importance of preserving their environment, business owners can take a leadership role in saving the earth. When businesses set sound environmental policies at the workplace, they also can influence the behavior of their employees at home. All business owners can step forward to meet this challenge. Not only because it's the right thing to do, but because saving the earth is good business.

Chapter 2

Recycling

"Recycling in many ways was the first and easiest area to make an impact."

Werner Braum
North America Senior Vice President
Ramada International Hotels & Resorts

"Recycling works because it's based on a cherished American principle: free enterprise."

William O. Bourke
Chairman and Chief Executive Officer
Reynolds Metals Company

"Recycling makes you feel good about yourself; like when you leave the blood bank."

Carole Newman
Speedy Print, Inc.

Most Americans grew up considering the United States to be the land of abundance. Perhaps that's why, until recently, they never gave much thought to throwing things away. With a cavalier attitude of "there's always more where that came from," our disposable society manages to send 450 million cubic yards of trash to the landfill every year. That's enough garbage to bury 26,000 football fields in a layer of garbage ten feet deep. According to the Waste Recyclers Council, that's enough trash to keep 50,000 trucks working daily to remove the refuse Americans toss away. An increasing awareness of the impact of trash on our environment, along with a severe and long lasting economic recession, has forced many Americans and most business owners to think twice about trash.

Most of what is found in the garbage bin at a business, as well as at home, can be salvaged, recycled and put to use, if these valuable materials can be intercepted before they reach the landfill. The most common resources businesses recycle today include paper, aluminum, glass, plastic and rubber tires. Some businesses have been successful in recycling oils, solvents, packaging materials, food, landscape debris and wood.

Recycling programs require three critical elements to be effective. First, they must be easy to implement. If the program is too complicated or requires too much effort, human nature will prevail and participation will not reach the level needed to make the program successful. Remember, getting people to recycle means having to break their lifelong habits of throwing everything away. Second, someone has to separate the recyclable materials from the garbage. Third, unless a market exists for the resources that are collected and separated, they have little value as a reusable commodity.

To make recycling work, business owners must make a conscious decision to buy recycled products whenever possible, even if they cost more. By stimulating demand in the marketplace for recycled goods, more will be produced. Competition will occur, technology will provide more efficient ways to generate new products from used resources, and the price of recycled goods will drop.

Purchasing recycled paper, for example, can have a dramatic effect on the environment. Every ton of recycled office paper saves approximately 17 trees, 4,100 kilowatts of energy (enough to power an average home for six months), 7,000 gallons of water, 60 pounds of pollutants from being released into the atmosphere and three cubic yards of landfill space. Actually, paper making and recycling in the United States have been linked for 300 years, since early paper was made from recycled fiber derived from cotton and linen rags. Now, it becomes important for our earth's future that we request and purchase recycled paper and other recycled products.

You might as well get your business started with a voluntary recycling program, because before long your company may be required by law to participate. According to the National Solid Waste Management Association, recycling laws are sweeping the nation. Many states have already enacted comprehensive recycling laws requiring detailed statewide recycling plans with incentives or penalties to stimulate compliance.

Is setting up a recycling program a good business decision? You bet! Thousands of companies are exploring recycling as a cost saving measure. Others are generating revenue by selling their recyclable materials. Just consider what the following businesses have accomplished.

Reynolds: First In Aluminum Recycling

Reynolds Metals Company, headquartered in Richmond, Virginia, is one of the world's largest fully-integrated aluminum producers. Reynolds pioneered the 12-ounce aluminum can in 1963 and consumer recycling of aluminum a few years later. Their recycling effort pays the public for their aluminum cans, then Reynolds melts the cans for use in new products. This process conserves natural resources and energy while forming a partnership with the American people to protect the nation's countryside from unsightly litter.

Reynolds opened the first of its own nationwide network of consumer recycling centers in California in 1968. To date, Reynolds has recycled more than 120 billion aluminum cans and has paid out more than $1.4 billion for metal that might otherwise be littering the nation's highways or loading up landfills. Recycling aluminum from cans and other sources saves 95 percent of the energy required to make aluminum from bauxite ore, conserving not only electricity, but also raw materials.

The beauty of Reynold's system, which operates more than 625 recycling centers and 100 automatic can recycling machines, as well as 26 processing plants across the country, is multifold: it prevents litter, reduces pressure on the landfills, rewards recycling with cash, conserves energy and preserves raw materials. The company's recycling program saves Reynolds hundreds of millions of dollars every year.

What's in it for Reynolds?

Reynolds has enjoyed tremendous corporate savings, and since 1968, also has generated consumer good will by paying $1.4 billion to the public for cans returned for recycling.

Red Lobster Saves Trees And Nets Dollars

Orlando-based Red Lobster U.S.A., the nation's largest seafood restaurant chain, has embarked on a recycling program that will eliminate enough trash to fill 1,000 eight-ton trash trucks annually. Utilized at nearly 500 Red Lobster restaurants across the country, the program will virtually prevent more than 16 million pounds of paper, cardboard, plastic, glass and other materials from ending up in landfills each year. These materials will be diverted from the waste stream and processed into usable items, thanks to the efforts of Red Lobster.

The initial step the restaurant chain has taken to implement their waste reduction program is to reduce the amount of trash generated at each location. To do this, Red Lobster restaurants nationwide have completely eliminated the use of paper napkins, paper rings and paper placemats. Instead, they are using linen napkins, which are laundered and reused. The policy of switching to linen napkins alone will save about 40,000 trees from being harvested annually for Red Lobster paper products. This also will remove 4.7 million pounds of paper from the waste stream each year.

Most of the company's restaurants collect and sort recyclable items that are picked up by local recycling organizations or trash haulers. To complete the recycling chain, the organizations or haulers sell those items to recycling processors, who, in turn, convert the waste back into reusable materials -- such as recycled paper, cardboard boxes and other items -- which then are sold back to Red Lobster and other companies.

By sending less trash to landfills, the company ultimately will spend less money on trash-hauling expenses and tipping fees, which are based on tonnage. Even after all costs associated with implementing the company's recycling program are paid, Red Lobster anticipates saving as much as $250,000 per year.

What's in it for Red Lobster, U.S.A.?

Red Lobster is making a contribution to safeguarding our environment, saving precious landfill space in the hundreds of communities it serves and achieving annual corporate savings of $250,000.

Baby Food Jars Get New Life At Car Colors Company

Jan Larkin, owner of Car Colors in Omaha, Nebraska, found that recycling baby food jars is the perfect way to save money and eliminate unnecessary waste. She collects the jars from customers, friends and relatives. Then, she fills them with small quantities of auto paint to be used for "touch up" jobs. When customers leave her auto supply shop, they also receive a small supply of matching paint to take care of that inevitable "ding" or dent. Reusing baby jars supplied at no cost eliminates the expense of purchasing other small containers.

Of course, Car Color's recycling efforts are not restricted to baby food jars. The company also saves used paint thinner in recycled 5-gallon cans, removes the paint and reuses the thinner or provides it to companies that can accept a lower grade product. In addition, they reuse corrugated boxes to avoid purchasing packing materials. Jan Larkin estimates that her overall reuse and recycling efforts save her company approximately $5,000 annually.

What's in it for Car Colors?

Annual savings of approximately $5,000 and the reuse of supplies that otherwise would end up in the landfill.

Speedy Print, Inc.: Feeling Good About Recycling

Printing press set up sheets, copying paper and printing paper are just some of the types of wastepaper generated at Speedy Print, Inc. in Nashville, Tennessee. Carole and Chet Newman, owners of this print shop, find themselves putting sizable quantities of this waste in a separate bin to be hauled away by a recycler.

Other recycling efforts include actively promoting the use of recycled paper at their small press print shop. They are happy to report that the customer demand is strong and recycled paper is successfully competing against paper manufactured from virgin wood pulp.

The shop also takes aluminum cans, glass and newspaper to neighborhood recycling bins twice a week. Funds earned from this form of recycling go to the Lake View Elementary School. As Carole Newman says; "Although our business doesn't make any money off recycling, it makes us feel good about ourselves. It's the same kind of feeling you get when you leave a blood bank."

What's in it for Speedy Print, Inc.?

Extra money for a local school, community goodwill and a great feeling.

Cartridgecare: The Business Of Recycling Can Turn Into A Business

Irene Conlan, of Scottsdale, Arizona's CartridgeCare, became interested in recycling laser printer toner cartridges when she had to throw her first one away. She says "pitching that cartridge made me feel like I was throwing away a car because it was out of gas. It not only seemed financially wasteful but, since the plastic cartridge is non-biodegradable and ends up in the trash, environmentally irresponsible as well."

In the Spring of 1989, Irene Conlan helped create CartridgeCare, a full-service, laser printer support company specializing in recycling toner cartridges. CartridgeCare collects the used cartridges and refurbishes them, then sells them at a considerable discount off the price of new ones. Since starting, it is estimated that the company has saved their customers more than $400,000 by remanufacturing and selling used laser printer cartridges. In addition, her efforts have kept approximately 20 tons of nonbiodegradable plastic out of the Phoenix/Scottsdale area landfills.

What's in it for CartridgeCare?

A successful new business grossing $600,000 in revenue annually and a reduction in the amount of trash sent to the landfill.

Giant Food, Inc.: A Giant Of A Recycler

Involving all 27,000 of its workforce associates, Washington, D.C.-based Giant Food, Inc. has undertaken a number of recycling programs within their more than 150 stores, offices and distribution center facilities.

Giant operates newspaper drop-off collection centers at 40 of its stores. The newspapers are recycled and the net profits are given back to the community in the form of grants to nonprofit, charitable organizations. Since the program's inception in 1976, Giant has given $168,000 back to the communities participating in its newspaper collection project.

In 1990, Giant began collecting plastic bags at 31 stores. The collected bags are bundled and then baled at the corporation's salvage facilities. Bags are then shipped to Mobil Corporation where they are made into other plastic products.

In addition, Giant has begun collecting aluminum soft drink cans from all store staff lounges. Collected cans are sent to their salvage warehouses, compacted and then picked up by a recycler. Profits from the sale of the cans are given to the United Way. Giant estimates that 92,000 pounds or 46 tons of cans are collected annually from their employee lounges.

Giant has been using retreaded truck tires for more than 20 years and finds them to be safe and reliable. By using retreaded truck tires, Giant realizes savings of $2,240 per tractor-trailer per year. Currently Giant operates a fleet of 300 tractors and 1,450 trailers. The savings are enormous.

Wooden pallets are used in warehousing operations to store and stack food commodities. By repairing more than 650,000 pallets annually, Giant avoids purchasing new wooden pallets and saves hundreds of trees. In addition, more than 66,000 pallets that are beyond repair are shipped for fuel and other uses.

Plastic film is used to wrap pallet loads of product to contain them during shipping. Within their warehousing operations, Giant recycles approximately 200 tons of plastic film wrap annually.

Giant's meat departments collect and recycle 20 million pounds of fat and bone annually. Bone and fat contain an oil called tallow, which is used in soapmaking production. Bone also is used as a protein ingredient for the agricultural feed industry.

Giant also recycles over 20,000 gallons of used motor oil annually from fleet maintenance operations.

What's in it for Giant Food, Inc.?

Although it is difficult for Giant to quantify the exact cost savings of their many environmental programs, the company knows that involvement in environmental activities is good for business, the community and for preserving natural resources.

Dollars For Denim Makes Big Bucks Selling Used Blue Jeans

Dollars For Denim, a Phoenix, Arizona company, exports 8,000 to 10,000 pairs of used blue jeans per month to customers in Japan and Western Europe. Laurie Olson, owner of the company, buys worn Levi's 501 jeans from thrift stores and directly from the public. She pays up to $10 a pair. The jeans are sorted and shipped from her reclamation center to overseas department stores and high fashion boutiques.

While Levi Strauss & Co., with manufacturing facilities in Belgium, France, Spain, Great Britain and the Philippines, can easily supply the world's demand for new jeans, foreigners crave the jeans made in America, especially the vintage 501's from the 1950s and 1960s. Young Japanese pay dearly for the jeans in an attempt to satisfy their fascination with American styles. Western Europeans also have a huge craving for the jeans, one that seems almost insatiable.

Ms. Olson's clothing recycling effort has blossomed into a substantial business. Dollars For Denim has monthly revenues running from $100,000 to $200,000.

What's in it for Dollars For Denim?

Monthly sales revenues of $100,000 to $200,000.

Eastman Kodak: A Companywide
Commitment To Recycling

Based in Rochester, New York, Eastman Kodak recycles numerous materials within its own manufacturing system, utilizing both sophisticated and relatively simple technologies. As a result, this $18 billion in sales company recycles 4.2 billion pounds of materials a year, making it one of the largest recyclers in the world.

Kodak has been recycling solvents and silver for more than 50 years. Every year, they recover and reuse more than 30 million troy ounces of silver derived from manufacturing film and photo paper. In addition, at least 30 million gallons of solvents are recovered annually, of which 600,000 gallons per year are sold to other companies for reuse. The remainder is used by Kodak. The company also recycles millions of pounds of cellulose acetate and other plastics, including x-ray film and worn and scratched motion picture film from theatres.

Waste materials such as various types of office paper, corrugated container-boards, plastic and metal are salvaged from Kodak's Rochester operations and sold to a recycler, accounting for approximately 65 million pounds per year. Using the methanolysis process, Kodak has been recycling more than 50 million pounds of polyethylene terephthalate (PET) plastic every year since 1976 and has recently been granted approval by the FDA to use recycled PET in polymer food-grade packaging. Eastman's Kodak Chemical Company is the worlds largest producer of bottle polymer. In 1992, Kodak's use of recycled bottle resin will account for recycling approximately 500 million 2-liter plastic beverage bottles which might otherwise go to the landfills.

Kodak also has developed programs aimed at post-consumer recycling. One program involves a closed-loop system to ensure the return of their disposable Fun Saver 35 cameras. The camera is engineered so that 85 percent of its parts can be recycled and reused. One hundred percent of the Kodak Fun Saver cameras being sold today contain plastic and metal recycled through this program. Other programs recycle film canisters, spools, steel magazines and other photographic waste.

What's in it for Eastman Kodak?

A recycling program that generates corporate savings of hundreds of millions of dollars per year.

Arizona Public Service: Serving The Environment Through Recycling

Arizona Public Service Company, Arizona's largest electric utility, has several types of recycling programs. The company, which is headquartered in downtown Phoenix, employs about 7,000 people throughout Arizona, and nearly half of those work in the Phoenix metropolitan area.

The utility's efforts at paper recycling began in 1979, when employees began placing computer paper in recycling bins. When the company relocated to its new headquarters building in 1989, employees received a different welcoming package as part of their new office furnishings -- two small paper bins, one for white and one for colored paper. Employees at other APS facilities also began separating their paper for recycling.

Today, bins containing dry trash are sent to a company that sorts and recycles nearly 65 percent of the company's waste. Reducing the amount of trash it sends to the landfill is a primary motivation for the recycling program. Although the utility doesn't make a profit on its paper recycling program, it expects these efforts to help stabilize disposal costs as landfill fees continue to increase.

For more than 20 years the utility has recycled scrap metal from the maintenance of thousands of miles of transmission and distribution lines, transformers, electric meters and other electrical equipment. Nearly 3 million pounds of scrap copper, aluminum and steel are accumulated each year from the wires, insulators, lightning arrestors, transformers, poles and other equipment. APS sells the scrap metal for more than $1 million per year.

As a statewide company, APS operates a fleet of more than 1,500 vehicles from large line trucks to passenger cars. Its transportation recycling efforts, including reusing containers for grease and recycling oil and air filters, are helping the company save money, as well as protecting the environment.

The fleet maintenance garage uses about 1,600 pounds of grease annually. By purchasing the grease in reusable lined containers and shipping its empty containers back to the oil company for refilling, APS is saving nearly 20 cents per pound. It also avoids the expense of disposing of empty grease drums. Used oil filters are crushed and recycled and air filters are sold to a local company that cleans them for resale.

What's in it for APS?

Revenue of more than $1 million per year, savings in the thousands and the minimizing of waste sent to landfills.

Frito-Lay, Inc.: Recycling Potato Chips As Cattle Feed

Way back in 1950, before the Frito-Lay name existed, the Dallas-based national food company was interested in preserving the environment. They noticed that about two percent of the corn in the company's grain elevator was discarded because the kernels were broken. In addition, since corn and potato chips are perishable food items, the company retrieved bags of chips that were close to losing their freshness on grocery store shelves. A livestock feeding program was developed to use the discarded corn and stale chips, thereby diverting these items away from landfills. The discarded corn is a primary source of livestock food at Frito-Lay's own experimental farm, while the stale chips are mixed with corn or other feed as a supplement.

Initiated over 40 years ago, this livestock feeding program has been expanded also to include potato and corn solids removed from the waste water of many of the company's manufacturing plants. As a result, more than 20 million pounds of potato and corn waste is recycled as cattle feed rather than ending up at the local dump.

What's in it for Frito-Lay?

Annual savings of $250,000 in livestock feed costs.

CBS Uses Colored Plastic Bags For Recycling

CBS Property Services, Inc., of Phoenix, Arizona, a residential and commercial real estate, brokerage, leasing and property management company, has initiated a Total Waste and Recovery Program with the help of Why Waste America, Inc. and Laidlaw Waste Systems. The project is in place at the CamelSquare office complex, which consists of 11 garden office buildings with 295,000 square feet of space. It is a workable program for all business tenants involved and is designed to reduce future recycling handling costs. The mechanics of the program are simple.

First, all recyclable items (magazines, junk mail, newspapers, paper, letterhead, soft drink cans, glass, aluminum, plastic with the recycle symbol and textiles) are placed in a clear plastic bag lining the trash cans by each desk. A large, black trash can is distributed to each office. This receptacle has a black plastic liner in it. Items that cannot be recycled (such as coffee grounds, food, wet and contaminated items) are placed in the black trash can with the black plastic liner. The janitorial staff retrieves the trash bags each evening and places them in the proper on-site trash bins for hauling. Only the black bags go to the landfill. The clear bags with the recycled items are diverted from the landfills and sent to a reclamation center.

What's in it for CBS Property Services, Inc.?

Lower costs to haul trash and a small income from selling recyclable items.

HOW YOUR BUSINESS CAN DO IT, TOO!

RECYCLING is not only good for the environment, it can also be good for your business. To determine how your business can get involved, first conduct an audit of your business operations to see what items can be reused within, traded, sold or otherwise diverted from the landfill. The amount of money that can be saved or generated by recycling depends on the volume and types of materials recycled.

Whenever possible, purchase supplies and business materials made from recycled resources. Increased demand for recycled products will not only lead to greater availability and lower prices, but will keep the recycling loop connected as well.

Put a ✔ in the box next to the activities you can implement in your daily business operations. Then, list them in the back of the book with other recycling efforts you discover.

☐ Scrap Paper

Designate a collection site(s) for recyclable paper. Next to the copy machine is an ideal location. If you have a large operation, put a collection site on every floor. Then, provide three bins marked "white paper," "colored paper" and "cardboard/newspapers."

Provide each employee with a small desktop container to collect recyclable paper. A simple box will do. When the containers are full, employees can dump the paper in the bins at the collection site. When the bins are full, they can be taken to a central storage area or pickup point.

Arrange with a paper collector to pickup the paper or drop it off at a local recycling center. If you have a small operation, you might consider joining with other occupants of your office building, shopping center or industrial park to set up a cooperative program. Ask your building manager for help.

☐ Cardboard Boxes

If your company receives products in cardboard or corrugated boxes, the boxes can be recycled as scrap or flattened, bundled and sold to companies that buy and sell used boxes. Boxes and other shipping materials also can be collected and reused for your own shipping needs. Some companies stamp the used boxes with a message such as "This box is being reused to save the environment."

☐ Scratch Pads

Eliminate the cost of buying scratch pads. Place a container next to the copy machine to collect all the bad copies, placing them in the container with the clean side up. Cut the sheets in half and staple together to use as scratch pads. After these pads are used, put the scratch paper into the recycle bins.

☐ Aluminum Cans

Set up recycle bins in employee cafeterias and lounges to capture all recyclable materials. Label the bins, "paper," "glass," or "aluminum cans," so employees can sort the items on the spot. Then, find the location of the most convenient aluminum can collection center. Check the Yellow Pages or state recycling office. Some organizations and recyclers pick up. Then, determine what form the cans must be in; most recycling centers prefer to accept flattened cans. Finally, decide where you're going to collect and store the cans until they're taken to a recycling center. If you have a soft drink machine, placing a large box or bin nearby would be ideal.

☐ Glass Containers

Check the Yellow Pages or state recycling office to locate the nearest glass recycling center. Then, find out if glass has to be separated by color to be accepted. Keep a large box or bin handy to collect bottles, jars, etc. Also, designate a storage area to collect glass until it is taken to a recycling center.

☐ Plastic

Plastic scrap -- computer ribbon cartridges, receptacles, office furniture -- often can be ground up and made into other products. As a result, certain forms of scrap plastic can earn businesses a tidy sum when recycled. Put up a sign informing employees of this fact. Keep a bin and/or area handy for storing plastic items to be scrapped. Check the Yellow Pages for a plastic recycling center.

☐ Packing Supplies

Recycle styrofoam peanuts. Rather than tossing them in the trash, save them in your shipping area and reuse them to safely pack your items that need shipping. Shred your waste paper and computer paper to make your own packing materials. Use paper packaging tape instead of plastic to make boxes easier to recycle. Reuse boxes, Manila envelopes and bubble bags whenever possible, using a rubber stamp to apply the message "We're reusing packing materials to help save the earth."

☐ Food

Some spoiled, stale and leftover food items from food processing companies or large food service firms can be recycled as feed for cattle, pigs and other livestock. Contact the local farm bureau for details. In most communities, leftover or excess food from restaurants or catered events can be donated to a shelter for the homeless or needy.

☐ Solvents

Some solvents, such as used paint thinner, can be collected, recycled or sold for other uses. If your company deals with solvents or other hazardous wastes, check with your local environmental agency to determine if you can collect and sell your used solvent to a recycling firm. If not, be sure to take special measures to dispose of them properly.

☐ Used Motor Oil

Look for service stations and repair shops that recycle motor oil and have your company cars and trucks serviced at these facilities. If you maintain your own fleet of vehicles, be sure to explore ways to capture and recycle all car fluids.

☐ Retreaded Tires

Consider replacing tires on company trucks, vans or cars with retreaded tires. Patronize service and repair centers that carry "recycled" tires and be sure to dispose of used tires at a tire recycling center. Recycled tires can be ground up and made into rubber flooring, new rubber products and asphalt. Some waste tires are being used to build artificial reefs in the ocean.

☐ Metals

Rather than dumping scrap metals in the garbage dumpster, salvage the metal and sell it to scrap metal dealers. Look in the Yellow Pages or call your local recycling center for more information.

☐ Buy Back Reusable Items From Your Customers

You may have items going out the door that could come back for reuse with a little customer encouragement. For example, a dry cleaner might offer to wash and press one shirt free of charge if the customer brings back a certain number of wire clothes hangers for reuse. The company saves money by not having to buy hangers and encourages customer loyalty and return business with the recycling effort.

☐ Toner Cartridges

Check your local market for a company that will buy back and recharge toner cartridges for your laser printers and copy machines.

Chapter 3

Conservation

"Waste not, want not."

John Platt

"Conserving energy and natural resources is a wise investment in our future and a way to improve the quality of our environment."

Mark De Michele
Chief Executive Officer and President
Arizona Public Service Company

"As a private citizen, I am an environmentalist; but, I also am the owner of a company. As a corporate citizen, I believe business owners need to get more involved with saving the earth."

Maurice Holloway
Chief Executive Officer
Cornnuts

"There's such a technological revolution in the pieces of the energy efficiency puzzle and how you put them together that the potential savings are more than two times as big and three times cheaper than they were five years ago."

Amory B. Lovins
Director of Research
Rocky Mountain Institute

Of all the ways your business can help save the earth, conservation is probably the one that can have the greatest impact on your bottom line. After all, if you conserve -- use less -- water, electricity or other fuels, your utility bills and energy costs will be lowered immediately. Likewise, if you use less materials and other supplies that often end up in the waste stream, your business can reduce its operating expenses.

Is conservation of our nation's water and energy the sole responsibility of business and industry? Definitely not! However, conservation measures adopted by business can lead the way and complement the conservation efforts of residential consumers. According to the Energy Information Administration, American industry consumes 37 percent of our country's electricity, petroleum and natural gas. Residential and commercial use accounts for another 36 percent, while transportation claims 27 percent. If individuals and businesses do their part, the earth's resources can be conserved for future generations.

Conservation is not new. Doing more with less always has been a practice of the thrifty-minded. But talk of carpooling, water conservation, alternative energy sources, energy efficient facilities and higher mileage vehicles only became part of everyday conversation and many companies' strategic planning when the first energy crisis hit in 1973.

Conservation measures put into place immediately after the Arab oil embargo were effective, but the intensity at which companies pursued resource and money-saving measures slackened when oil prices dropped. The bottom line benefits of conservation are once again spurring American business into action. Part of this renewed interest is driven by government regulations or incentives. Other companies are responding to consumers' demands to do their part to help save the earth and its finite resources.

Whatever the motivation, conservation truly is a "win-win" strategy for American business and the nation. Businesses will lower their expenses, less pollution will be generated, and reliance on imported fuels will decrease.

How can your business conserve resources and save money? Just take a look at what some other companies have done.

Sheraton Society Hill : An Environment Friendly Hotel

The Sheraton Society Hill Hotel in Philadelphia is not only concerned with the satisfaction of their customers, it also is concerned with being environmentally conscious. The hotel's general manager, Fred Corso, says "the Sheraton Society Hill wants to become the city's first environment friendly hotel."

In order to conserve energy, the hotel uses energy saving shower heads which reduce the flow of hot water. They also have installed fluorescent light bulbs, which require less electricity, throughout the hotel. Another conservation measure the hotel is exploring is the use of infrared sensors, which send signals to automatically turn on the heat or air conditioning when a person enters the room and automatically shutdown the system when the person leaves. This effort is expected to reduce the amount of unnecessary energy used to heat or cool empty rooms and will save money which can be used in other ways for the comfort of the hotel guests.

Sheraton's environmental efforts also include recycling food waste, office paper, newspaper, corrugated cardboard, aluminum cans, glass, plastic and tin cans.

The Sheraton Society Hill Hotel management believes that, in addition to saving money and protecting the environment, conservation and recycling are just good business practices. Randi Millstein, of the Sheraton Systems Department, believes that "It makes you feel better to know that we're doing this. I'm proud of our hotel."

What's in it for the Sheraton Society Hill Hotel?

Satisfied customers, committed employees and energy savings of $10 - $12,000 annually.

Frito-Lay: Cogeneration Used To Produce Energy

Frito-Lay has realized the need to protect our planet and preserve our natural resources for future generations. One plant in Bakersfield, California produces its own energy through cogeneration, one of the most energy-efficient means of power generation. Through this process, natural gas is burned to produce steam and electricity. The steam is used to produce snacks and the electricity is used to power the plant for production. Not only does this process provide electricity for Frito-Lay, but a local utility company also benefits because the excess electricity is sold to them.

Frito-Lay is always on the look out for technology that will allow their plants to reduce energy usage. They have developed several programs which have helped reduce, by 1.3 percent, the amount of energy used over the past year. For example, a plant in Frankfort, Indiana reuses waste heat from the potato chip cooking operation to heat up the building. This single effort alone reduces Frito-Lay's fuel needs by 400,000 gallons of oil a year. Another effort includes the use of propane-powered sales vehicles. The vehicles offer a clean alternative to gasoline powered ones by eliminating carbon particulates from vehicle emissions and reduce dependence on foreign oil.

Frito-Lay currently is in the process of conserving water through a program at their manufacturing facilities which is expected to reduce water usage by up to one billion gallons over a three-year period. But conservation for Frito-Lay doesn't stop here. They have been following environmentally sound practices for about 40 years and intend to continue exploring many new opportunities.

What's in it for Frito-Lay?

Reduction of fuel needs by 70 billion BTUs of energy in one year, leading to a 630,000 gallon decrease in Frito-Lay's need for oil and saving the company $450,000.

Devman Company Saves Energy And Reduces Costs Of Lighting Medical Buildings

The Phoenix-based DevMan Company is a full-service real estate brokerage firm that specializes in providing property management, development, sales and leasing services to owners of medical care facilities. They manage more than 400,000 square feet of medical office space and have found that changing lighting fixtures can reduce operational costs and save energy.

By replacing incandescent light fixtures with fluorescent fixtures and fluorescent retrofit kits, the DevMan Company has been able to significantly reduce the operational costs of lighting and cooling the buildings it manages. A fluorescent flood light fixture, for example, has a much longer life span - lasting up to five times longer than incandescent flood lights. This not only saves the cost of replacement lamps, it also saves the labor and maintenance costs of replacing them. In areas where light fixtures are hard to reach, such as exterior lighting on second and third floors, maintenance costs can be high if a scissor lift or other equipment must be rented to change the bulbs.

Fluorescent lamps also use less energy, yet generate the same amount of light. In addition, they burn cooler, thus reducing inside air conditioning needs which are significant in medical facilities where more lighting usually is required, or in warm climates where air conditioning is a must.

Upgrading existing fluorescent fixtures with new technology, such as electronic ballasts, also can reduce energy usage. The electronic ballasts generate less heat which gives them a longer life span and also lowers air conditioning costs. Fluorescent flood lamps for exterior and interior lighting are available as a complete individual system containing an aluminized glass reflector, a ballast adapter and a fluorescent lamp. These preassembled units simply screw into any standard incandescent socket, making installation easy.

In addition to general office lighting, the DevMan Company is in the process of retrofitting all indoor "exit" signs to fluorescent bulbs to achieve additional savings. Since these signs stay on 24 hours a day, seven days a week, the savings are expected to be significant.

"In our experience, we have generally recaptured our investment in the new, more expensive lighting fixtures in the first year. Savings in future years are expected to be significant. A recent retrofit of an 1,800 square foot medical suite which had an inordinate amount of incandescent flood lights, for example, will yield savings of about $1,500 per year," said William E. Molloy, DevMan partner.

What's in it for the buildings managed by the DevMan Company?

Reduction of energy use and maintenance savings of thousands of dollars annually.

Security Pacific Bank Lowers Maintenance Costs While Saving Precious Water In Southwest States

Security Pacific Bank, which has nearly 900 branch offices in six Western states, realized in 1989 that xeriscaping could have dramatic results for its operations in Arizona and Nevada.

Although both states have a desert climate, many of the branches in those locations had lush green landscaping. With an eye toward conserving water and reducing costs for water and landscaping maintenance, the decision was made to convert nearly 100 locations to desert landscaping.

"We expected desert landscaping to cut our water usage by 75 percent," said David Ray, first vice president and southwest regional manager of Real Estate Asset Management for Security Pacific. "With all the attention to water conservation, we felt we were setting a precedent by taking steps to dramatically reduce our bank's consumption."

Water conservation is becoming an ever more pressing issue in Arizona, Nevada, California and other states in the western part of the country. Some cities have already enacted ordinances to reduce water consumption. Tougher measures are sure to follow. Desert landscaping, or xeriscaping, offers a solution with multiple benefits. In addition to reducing water consumption, xeriscaping dramatically reduces the associated maintenance costs of lawn mowing, replacing broken sprinkler heads, and other costs such as fertilizing and planting of seasonal grasses.

The change at Security Pacific Bank has added up to impressive savings. On average, water consumption at each branch location was cut by 450,000 gallons, resulting in a $243 annual reduction in water bills and $1,740 in maintenance costs at each site. Despite the costs of converting lush landscaping to xeriscaping, Security Pacific has already recouped its investment.

What's in it for Security Pacific Bank?

A reduction in total water and maintenance costs from $518,940 in 1987 to $290,425 in 1990.

Cornnuts Harvests Savings In Operations

Cornnuts, a family-owned company in Oakland, California that has been in business since 1936, has followed its environmental conscience for nearly 20 years. Environmental concerns have helped shape Cornnuts' agricultural, manufacturing and administrative operations in many different ways.

Cornnuts, tasty oversized roasted corn kernels, are not as simple to produce as they look. The present day snack is made from a hybrid corn developed after years of testing. Corn geneticists began working in 1959 to develop a hybrid similar to the original "Cuzco" corn that was imported exclusively from Peru to make Cornnuts.

Cornnuts' first proprietary giant hybrid corn was produced in 1964, and several subsequent hybrids have been introduced since. The present hybrid, which matures sooner and dries more quickly than the others, can be grown using approximately 12 percent less irrigation water, compared to the original hybrid.

The corn harvesting industry realized a significant technological advancement in 1979, which provided Cornnuts with the opportunity to replace its existing harvesting system with picker-sheller combines. The new combines, which pick, shuck, and shell the corn in the field, increased harvesting capacity by five times per machine. Cornnuts subsequently installed a new drying facility to accommodate this new technology, and decreased drying time from five days to five hours. This new process reduced Cornnuts' consumption of electricity and natural gas by 90 percent per ton of corn.

Cornnuts introduced its first drip irrigation system in 1990 in California, where most of its corn is grown. It also is preparing to help its growers convert to drip irrigation for their crops. Through this change, Cornnuts hopes to achieve a 66 percent reduction in its water usage.

Cornnuts' concern for the environment doesn't stop out in the field. Its new processing and manufacturing plant in Fresno, California, was built from the ground up with energy conservation in mind. A computerized energy management system controls the environment within the plant to maximize the energy sensitive design of the building. For example, heat from the boiler room warms adjacent rooms in the winter. Evaporative coolers in the kitchen provide energy efficient cooling in the summer.

The warehouse was designed for passive heating and cooling. And, since large quantities of water are used in processing the corn, several water conservation systems were built into the plant.

Employees at each of Cornnuts' three California locations are involved in other environmental programs created by employee environmental committees. Cornnuts also recycles all paper products, laser printer toner cartridges, glass, aluminum and cardboard, and uses recycled paper. Disposable items have been eliminated from the company's employee kitchens and Cornnuts invites its 230 employees to bring their recyclables to work for pick up by the company recycler.

What's in it for Cornnuts?

As a result of their overall efforts, Cornnuts pays lower utility bills today than they did 12 years ago, despite substantially increased production. Cornnuts also enjoys the satisfaction of meeting its mission statement, which includes a promise to foster integrity regarding product, people and the environment.

The Wigwam Resort: Switching On Hot Water Through Previously Wasted Energy

In 1988, Arizona Public Service Company (APS) presented a proposal to the Wigwam Resort that would utilize previously wasted energy to meet a significant portion of the resort's hot water needs. The 60-year old Wigwam resort, a 241-room, internationally-known, five-star resort and country club located in Litchfield Park, Arizona, undertook renovation involving the addition of a new laundry facility, swimming pool and spa. As a result of these changes, higher energy bills were anticipated.

In addition, the resort's air-conditioning system consisted of two commercial chillers which were old and unreliable, and renovation plans did not involve replacement of the chillers. Since the resort planned to remain open during the summer of 1989 for the first time, and summertime temperatures generally range from 100-115° F, it was questionable as to whether the resort's existing air-conditioning unit could meet these new cooling requirements.

Most commercial facilities heating and air conditioning systems not only reject heat which is a byproduct of their refrigeration system, they also pay for the energy (usually natural gas) used to heat water. The Wigwam Resort was no exception. The chillers absorbed heat from inside the buildings and discharged it into the atmosphere. APS's plan involved the use of a heat recovery system, the first of its kind in Arizona, through which waste heat derived from an industrial heat pump was used to meet the additional water heating needs of the new swimming pool, spa and a portion of the laundry service. In addition, the chilling abilities of the heat pump would supplement the existing chillers.

The heart of the system is a 170-ton heat pump which operates as a lead chiller for the chilled water system, supplying 45-50°F water. As a byproduct, the heat pump also supplies 125° F water to the three plate and frame heat exchangers which pre-heat the laundry water to 120° F, the spa water to 105° F, and the pool water to 85° F.

A cooling tower was added to the hot water loop to make the heat pump's full capacity available during the summer season when extra cooling is required. As a result of the two byproducts supplied by the system, the Wigwam Resort was more responsive to the guests' needs for cool facilities and hot water, while at the same time making optimal use of the resort's energy.

By conserving 116,000 therms of natural gas, the Wigwam was able to save $61,000 per year. The equipment conversion project necessary to achieve this reduction in energy costs had a simple payback of 3.56 years.

What's in it for the Wigwam Resort?

Savings of $61,000 per year and plenty of hot water to keep guests and staff happy!

Winn-Dixie: Definitely Serious About Saving The Earth And Conserving Resources

When it comes to practicing innumerable and varied environmental measures, Jacksonville, Florida based Winn-Dixie supermarkets are definitely out in the forefront. Many of their innovative measures fall into the "Why didn't I think of that?" category.

For instance, equipment and parts for routine maintenance of stores and offices are ordered uncrated or unpacked whenever possible, and reused if appropriate, providing the used parts do not affect operational efficiency. Other measures are definitely on the cutting edge; for instance, the company was a leader in introducing stay-on tabs for company produced Chek beverage cans in 1976, thereby removing aluminum ring pulls from the waste stream. In 1991, they introduced photodegradable, "Easy Open Tear Tab" carriers for their Chek beverages to replace the plastic ring holders that are not biodegradable and often pose a hazard to wildlife.

Winn-Dixie's energy conservation program is aimed at achieving optimum efficiency and eliminating waste in all areas. Purchasing the most energy-efficient equipment is one step the company has taken; for instance, equipment was installed to reclaim rejected heat from refrigeration systems to provide both air temperature comfort and water heating. The use of computer controlled and monitored refrigeration and air conditioning systems also saves energy. While maintaining acceptable light levels, the use of reflectorized lighting reduces the amount of lamps and ballasts needed by about 50 percent.

Other steps include monitoring utility bills to guard against excessive use, increasing building insulation and decreasing building surface glass. To encourage and maintain employee awareness, an energy conservation awareness training video was created for retail associates. Also, awareness posters and stickers were put on walls and near equipment switches. Oil was conserved when their backhaul program was implemented and more than 802,000 miles were saved by their delivery tractor trailer fleet .

To reduce waste and conserve resources used in packaging, Winn-Dixie is taking several steps. First, most produce is available to customers in bulk, not prepackaged. In their offices, all documents are reproduced front and back to conserve paper use. Computer paper reports are downsized, consolidated and/or eliminated. In addition, an electronic mail system has been established throughout company offices to reduce paper usage. Packaging is being reduced on all private label products such as paper towels, bath tissue, napkins, paper plates, detergents and cracker boxes. Small boxes are being reused to pack customers' purchased products rather than using paper bags.

Winn-Dixie also has made many efforts in the recycling area. Scraps of fat and bone from the meat department are utilized in animal food. Used deli cooking oils are utilized in soapmaking. Egg cartons are made from recycled material and are recyclable after use. Company letterhead is printed on recycled paper, and silver is reclaimed from film processing in the company's photographic department. Reusable produce crates, lugs and hampers are returned to growers and farmers. Wooden pallets in the distribution center are repaired for reuse, thus helping to save trees. Nonrepairable wooden pallets are returned to crate builders for recycling.

"Recycling and conservation are the right things to do, from both a business and ecology point of view. Neither requires any real sacrifice for the company, so obviously helping to protect the environment is an all around good thing," said G.E. "Mickey" Clerc, vice president of Winn-Dixie.

What's in it for Winn-Dixie?

Aside from goodwill and a sense of achievement acquired through Winn-Dixie's multifaceted energy saving, resource conserving and recycling programs, they are sure their environmental awareness programs also have brought financial benefits to the company.

HOW YOUR BUSINESS CAN DO IT, TOO!

CONSERVATION should be a key word in the mission statement of every business. Conserving energy, natural resources and consumable items that often end up in the landfill is a smart thing to do; it saves money and helps to preserve and protect the earth. To get started with a conservation program for your company, conduct a complete review of your business operations and determine what specific things your business can do to conserve energy and cut back on consumable items, especially those made from nonrenewable resources.

The amount of money that can be saved through conservation depends on the commitment employees are willing to make toward taking simple steps in the workplace. Some savings, however, will be derived only by investing in new equipment or state-of-the-art technology. To determine if these investment measures are right for your company, you should get the advice of experts in the field that can provide a professional assessment. The point is, your company should look for ways to continue to meet market demand for your goods and services, while making a conscious effort to do everything possible to conserve.

Put a ✔ in the box next to the activities you can implement in your daily operations. Then, list them in the back of the book.

☐ Use Both Sides Of The Paper

Use both sides of a piece of paper and you'll reduce your paper expense by one-half. Encourage all your employees to copy and print on both sides of the paper. Post signs by the copy machine and announce the policy at staff meetings. In addition, keep a box by the copy machine for papers with mistakes. Use these pieces of paper for preparing drafts or for scratch paper.

☐ Turn It Off

Turn off equipment that is not in use. Turn off lights at the end of the work day. These simple activities can save your company hundreds of dollars in utility bills. Copiers, laser printers, coffee pots and other electrical equipment and appliances use considerable energy and often generate heat that impacts your building's cooling requirements. Put awareness posters or stickers near equipment switches. Designate an employee to be responsible for making sure that all equipment is turned off when not in use. If that doesn't work, put timers on the major equipment that will automatically turn off the machines during nonbusiness hours.

☐ Adjust The Thermostat

Adjust the thermostat up or down to save energy on cooling and heating when the facility is not in use. Designate an employee to be responsible for adjusting the thermostat at the end of each work day, or invest in a time control thermostat that automatically adjusts the system. Also, lower the thermostat on your business hot water heater to 130° .

☐ Eliminate Extra Copies

Encourage employees to conserve paper by not making extra, unnecessary copies of reports, memos or file copies. Route the same memo, rather than making a copy for everyone. Stick announcements on a bulletin board by the coffee pot or another common area. Determine, in advance, the minimum number of people that must receive a copy of a document and try to eliminate sending copies to individuals who could do without. Make only the exact number of copies necessary to achieve your desired communications. Explore the use of electronic mail, voice mail or other methods of communicating without paper.

☐ Change Lighting Fixtures

Do a lighting audit of your facility and determine if you could achieve savings by making an investment in new or adapted lighting fixtures. Changing lighting fixtures from incandescent to fluorescent can reduce operational costs by saving on the number of bulbs used, the energy consumed and the maintenance costs for bulb replacement. Reflectorized lighting can reduce the amount of lamps and ballasts needed by almost 50 percent. Change to fluorescent lights in your "exit" signs and convert 4-bulb fluorescent lighting fixtures to high efficiency 2-bulb fixtures.

☐ Eliminate Unnecessary Vehicle Trips

Save gas, oil and employee time by eliminating unnecessary trips in company or employee vehicles. Encourage employees to use the telephone, fax machine or electronic mail to communicate with associates, customers, vendors and suppliers, rather than drive across town for a meeting. Schedule deliveries to assure efficiency and to keep gasoline consumption to the minimum. Replace aging vehicles with smaller cars and vans that consume less fuel. Encourage employees to carpool, ride share, ride a bike or use public transportation to get to work.

☐ Purchase Energy Efficient Equipment

Before making an equipment purchasing decision, determine the energy efficiency of the product along with its potential life span. Select copiers and other equipment with power saver features. Many laptop and notebook computers now have the same power and capabilities as the traditional desk top PC and use as little as one percent of the energy required by a PC.

☐ Reflective Film

Adding reflective film or solar shade screens to your business windows can dramatically reduce summertime cooling costs.

☐ Check Your Facility For Energy Conservation

By adding insulation or by decreasing building surface glass, many older buildings can become more energy efficient. Do an energy audit or contract with an expert to determine the most cost-effective approach you can take to reduce the energy consumption of your facility and to lower your energy costs.

☐ Check Your Restrooms

Lots of savings can be made in facility restrooms. Check them frequently to make sure the sinks and toilets are not leaking. Use low-flow aerators or automatic shut-offs in the sinks and install toilet dams. Install electric hand dryers or cloth towel dispensers to eliminate paper towels which consume trees and end up in the landfill.

☐ Landscape Your Facility With Low-Water Use Plants

Convert your landscaping to xeriscaping or low-water use plants. You'll save money on your water bill and on landscape maintenance. Also, water your landscaping in early morning or evening to reduce evaporation.

☐ Check Your Air Filters

Dirty air filters can restrict the flow of warm and cool air through your ventilation system, causing the system to work harder and your utility bills to increase. Changing the filters regularly can be a low-cost preventive measure that also can improve indoor air quality.

☐ Maintain Your Heating & Cooling System

Have your entire heating and cooling system checked by a qualified professional annually. Heating and cooling costs have a huge impact on your utility expenses. A heating or cooling system that is not operating efficiently can use twice as much energy as one that has been properly maintained.

Chapter 4

Pollution And Toxin Elimination

"First, business goals and environmental goals do not always have to be in conflict. Pollution is waste, and waste is bad for productivity, just as it is bad for the environment."

Allen Jacobson
Retired Chairman & CEO
3M

"The development of a competitive, electronic-auto industry will do more to reduce oil imports than rigid fuel-efficiency standards ...."

President George Bush

"Winning the battle against air pollution is going to take the best efforts of everyone who can make a contribution."

Lodwrick M. Cook
Chairman & CEO
ARCO

Early man never worried about how to protect the environment so he could live in a world free of pollutants and toxins -- the air was clear and the water pure. Food, shelter and survival were the all consuming concerns of earth's early inhabitants, humans who experienced many hardships on their march to civilization.

While the industrial and technological advances of mankind have brought us comforts, conveniences and longevity, they also have brought us a polluted world. Now our concerns also include what to do about the impact on the environment from acid rain, ozone depletion, global climate change, agricultural chemicals, toxic substances, hazardous waste, radiation and contaminated water supplies.

Business and industry often are blamed for mankind's 20th century environmental ills, but returning to a pre-industrial lifestyle and economy is not an option. Current and future generations must wrestle with the dilemma of how to advance civilization, while at the same time preserve and protect the earth.

Pollution prevention, a strategy fundamentally different from pollution control and waste management, is the preferred method in the hierarchy of environmental practices. Pollution prevention is a simple concept. It means taking measures to address pollution at its source of generation, rather than trying to manage, control or clean it up afterwards. Preventing pollution leads to other economic benefits, such as reduced treatment and disposal costs, reduced liabilities, and potential savings on raw materials.

Substantial legislation to ensure compliance with measures to protect our earth has been enacted over the past three decades. At the federal level, there has been the Wilderness Act, the Clean Air Act, the Clean Water Act, the Safe Drinking Water Act, the Pollution Prevention Act, the Resource Conservation and Recovery Act and the Superfund, among others.

Countless environmental measures have become laws in all 50 states, and millions of people, representing regulatory agencies, science, industry, education and grass roots environmental movements, are involved in tackling today's environmental issues. Governments are devising incentives to help individuals and business leaders change the way that raw materials and goods are produced, consumed and disposed. Moreover, the educational system is beginning to teach our children lessons about earth care, lessons that older generations never regarded as necessary until recently.

The debate rages as to whether or not our environmental protection efforts are working, but one fact cannot be disputed -- more needs to be done. Our progress since the Clean Air Act of 1970 has been praised by some, and criticized by others as too slow. For example, although particulates, sulfur dioxide and carbon monoxide emissions fell between 1975 and 1984, improving urban air quality across the country, many categories of air pollutants today still exceed 66 percent of the 1970 levels. In addition, while significant progress has been made in the water quality of places such as Lake Erie, Puget Sound and the Chesapeake Bay, other streams and rivers remain polluted. Nevertheless, overall public awareness and interest in the environment have increased. People are changing their habits and, as a result, they also are expecting business to respond to their concerns about the environment.

"Green" marketing and going "green" by controlling or eliminating pollutions and toxins at your business are strategies which may help your company survive, as well as help the environment. The following case studies show what some companies are doing to keep our environment clean by reducing or eliminating pollution and toxins from their daily operations.

OxiSolv Closes The Loop On Water Usage

OxiSolv Corporation, an automobile restoration facility located in Blaine, Minnesota, makes significant use of water in its daily operations. Finding a way to reuse the rinse water, which is contaminated during the process by both organic compounds and metals, was a challenge met with the help of the Minnesota Office of Waste Management, an agency that provides techinical expertise and grant programs for innovation in the prevention and reduction of industrial pollution.

A filtration system has been devised that enables OxiSolv to reuse 300 gallons of water a day that formerly was sent down the sewers, and eliminates the pollutants from entering the water supply. The cost of this system, including installation, was approximately $5,100, compared to an estimated $18,000 to $22,000 for a conventional commercial system. Supply and waste disposal costs are about $90 per month.

"Not only has OxiSolv adopted this system to lessen the amount of pollution entering the environment," said Glenn Knowlton, of OxiSolv. "It also is safer for the work environment and our employees."

Using this new system at OxiSolv, the rinse water is first drained into a primary collector, where the largest particles are removed. The water is then pumped into a screen basket at the top of a large settling tank. In the settling tank, a flocculent is used to help settle out and remove some of the fine particles along with some of the heavy metals.

In the next step, the rinse water is pumped through an earth filter, where more of the fine sediment is removed. It is then pumped through two banks of sediment filters, and finally through a charcoal filter before being returned to the rinse tank for reuse.

What's in it for OxiSolv?

The company saved nearly $15,000 in the development costs of its filtration system. It also uses 300 less gallons of water each day, reducing its water bill. At the same time, its new process prevents industrial pollution at the source and helps keep the water supply clean.

3M: Worldwide Recognition, World Class Savings

As one of the nation's leading "blue-chip" companies, St. Paul, Minnesota- based 3M develops and manufactures more than 60,000 products for business, industry, government and consumers around the world. The company's "Pollution Prevention Pays" program, an industrial environmental conservation initiative that was begun in 1975, has been recognized the world over for its achievements.

3M's primary goal is to prevent pollution at the source of its products' manufacturing processes, rather than remove pollution after it has already been created. At best, conventional pollution-removal facilities will only temporarily constrain a problem, not eliminate it, which is the objective of "Pollution Prevention Pays."

While the idea itself is not new, the application of pollution prevention on a companywide basis, through a globally organized effort and recording the results, had not been done before. The dramatic results demonstrate the environmental impact and financial rewards of such efforts. Over the 16 years that the 3P program has been in existence (1975-1991), it has managed to cut 3M's pollution per unit of production in half.

The results of the 3P Program in the U.S. between 1975 and 1990 are as follows:

Pollution Prevented:

Air pollutants	120,000 tons
Water pollutants	15,600 tons
Wastewater	1 billion gallons
Sludge/solid waste	410,000 tons

These figures represent first year savings for each of the 3,000 3P projects totalled for each category.

The company's 3P program is a continuing effort, which focuses on eliminating pollution sources through product reformulation, process modification, equipment redesign, recycling and the recovery of waste materials for resale. Pollutants eliminated or reduced at the source under the 3P program include hydrocarbons (which contribute to ozone and smog), odor, contaminated water, dissolved solids, sulfur, zinc, alcohol and incinerated scrap. Before receiving the corporate blessing, all environmental projects designed to eliminate or reduce pollution must meet the following guidelines:

* Through process changes, product reformulation or other preventive means, elimination or reduction of a currently problematic pollutant or a pollutant that has the potential to become a 3M problem in the future is possible.

* In addition to reducing pollution, environmental benefits are exhibited through the reduction of energy consumption, more efficient use of raw materials, and improvement in the use of other natural resources.

* It should involve a technical accomplishment, innovative approach or unique design in meeting its objective.

* It must have some monetary benefit to 3M. This may be through reduced or deferred pollution control or manufacturing costs, increased sales of an existing or new product, or other reductions in capital or expenses.

Among the 785 3P projects in the United States is a project at a 3M facility in Alabama that is concerned with recycling cooling water that had previously been collected for disposal with wastewater. Reusing the cooling water has allowed 3M to scale down the capacity of a planned wastewater treatment facility from 2,100 to 1,000 gallons per minute. The recycling facility cost $480,000, but 3M saved $800,000 on the construction cost alone.

Another project involved the redesign of a resin spray booth which had been producing about 500,000 pounds of overspray per year that required special incineration disposal. New equipment was installed to provide a net reduction in the total amount of resin, saving more than $125,000 annually on a $45,000 equipment investment. While savings realized by individual 3P programs are impressive, the total savings are truly dramatic; over $500 million!

What's in it for 3M?

Over $500 million in corporate savings and recognition for its aggressive efforts to be responsive to the needs of the environment throughout its manufacturing process.

Fetzer Vineyards: Leading The Way With Organic Farming

Fetzer Vineyards, located in Mendocino County, California, has taken risky yet successful steps towards revolutionizing American winemaking by ridding its vineyards of pesticides, herbicides and fungicides. This family-owned vineyard, started in 1968 by Barney Fetzer, his wife, Kathleen, and their 11 sons and daughters, began by experimenting with an organically grown fruit and vegetable garden in 1985. The results were impressive.

John Fetzer, chief executive; James, president; and Mary, marketing director, decided to try organic gardening in the vineyards as well. They reasoned that if the winery could raise grapes organically, it would lower costs, protect its workers from exposure to chemicals, prevent water and soil pollution, and answer the public's growing desire for food and beverages that are free of chemicals.

Since it was a risky proposition, Fetzer decided to convert one parcel of the 1,000 plus acres of vineyard to organic farming at a time, as long as the benefits outweighed the risks. In 1988, the home-ranch vineyard, a 131-acre parcel and the first Fetzer vineyard, was completely freed of pesticides, herbicides and fungicides.

Skeptics in the industry waited for the vineyard to be tormented by bugs and mold, but that did not happen. The harvest of Cabernet Sauvignon, Sauvignon Blanc and Zinfandel grapes was normal, and projections indicated that the costs associated with using organic methods would decrease in future years. Over the next two years, another 350 acres were converted to organic viniculture. By 1990, Fetzer had committed itself to growing all its grapes organically by converting 100 to 200 acres annually and farming the other vineyards with transitional organic and Integrated Pest Management (IPM) methods. It is now the largest major winery in the country that has pledged to grow all of its grapes organically.

"Growing organic grapes is a marketing gimmick, and it's what we believe in," said James Fetzer. "When we started the garden, our sales people thought we were nuts, but I think we have created something experiential that educates people about food, literally from the ground up. Even if we could make more money by going on with (chemical) spraying, we'd be stupid to do so. Because, as a farmer, you're only as rich as your land is healthy."

What's in it for Fetzer?

Fetzer has received recognition as the leader in organic viniculture by sticking to their philosophical commitment to protect the earth and the health of the community, its children and the employees of Fetzer. Immediate benefits have been realized through lower workers compensation insurance costs and reduced risk of environmental lawsuits. In the long run, once capital equipment expenses are retired and adjustments to the process have been made during the transition period, Fetzer expects to enjoy considerable production savings.

Buckles Greenbelt Plants Clean The Air

Buckles Greenbelt, a 17-year-old Phoenix, Arizona company that specializes in designing interior plantscapes, is helping to clear the air about the benefits of adding greenery to businesses, homes and office buildings. Its work can be seen at the new Terminal 4 at Sky Harbor International Airport in Phoenix and in Biosphere II, the two-year controlled environment experiment located outside of Tucson, Arizona.

"Plants oxygenate the air. They literally clean the air by digesting benzene, tricholoroethylene and formaldehyde," said Michael Buckles, owner and president of the company. "Without plants, our planet would not survive."

According to Buckles Greenbelt, a National Aeronautics and Space Administration (NASA) research scientist discovered that the air in an average 1,800 square-foot home can be freshened and cleaned by installing 15 to 20 golden pathos and spider plants. Plants also can alleviate the "sick-building" syndrome by cleaning the air of pollutants.

Concern about interior air pollution has accelerated since most new buildings have few windows or windows that do not open. The concern has been the springboard for a new industry dedicated to maximizing the effectiveness of plants indoors as a solution to indoor air pollution. New techniques, such as designing a planter with a small fan and charcoal filter at the bottom, can help a plant work more effectively by drawing pollutants like cigarette smoke and pollen through the leaves.

Buckles Greenbelt is a founding member of the Foliage for Clean Air Council, a member of the Interior Plantscape Division of the Associated Landscape Contractors of America, and is participating with NASA in a two-year study on the effectiveness of plants in cleaning the air inside buildings, including future space stations.

"With all the interest in environmental concerns like air pollution, plants are being recognized for their function as well as their beauty," Buckles said. "They are the ultimate clean-air machine because they are clean, quiet and effective."

What's in it for Buckles Greenbelt?

A booming business in indoor plant landscaping grossing $250,000 in annual sales. In addition, recognition as a company looking for natural solutions to dealing with pollution problems.

Warner-Lambert: Preventing Pollution Is Company's Goal

Headquartered in Morris Plaines, New Jersey, Warner-Lambert is committed to assuming a leadership role in business and industry through their efforts to help protect our earth and the people who inhabit it. The following are only a few of the steps they have taken.

Warner-Lambert is one of an initial 18 participants in the Green Lights Program sponsored by the Environmental Protection Agency (EPA). The Green Lights Program since has been expanded to include 160 participants. The goal of the program is to improve the environment through energy efficiency. The program involves retrofitting in- efficient lighting systems to meet new standards, as well as designing new construction to provide efficient lighting.

Within a five-year period, Warner-Lambert also expects to have reduced their air emissions for carbon dioxide, sulphur dioxide and nitrogen oxide by 20,000, 140, and 75 tons per year, respectively. This reduction is a result of the participation by Warner-Lambert in the Green Lights Program.

Pollution prevention is the goal at Warner-Lambert. All underground fuel and oil tanks have been replaced with protected tanks that are designed to prevent potential sources of groundwater pollution. Thermal oxidation systems have been installed to capture air pollutants from several production processes. These systems have resulted in a 240,000-pound per year reduction in pollutants released into the atmosphere. In addition, boilers at one of the company's plants utilize spent solvents instead of fossil fuel in the form of natural gas during power and steam production. Burning the solvents saves money and reduces demand for nonrenewable fossil fuels.

What's in it for Warner-Lambert?

Nearly 300,000 gallons of recovered solvents were burned in 1990, saving 35.5 million cubic feet of natural gas, or enough energy to supply 250 homes annually. Fuel savings also resulted in lower company fuel bills.

Arizona Public Service Pioneers Electric Cars While Reducing Pollutants From Gas-Powered Fleet

Arizona Public Service Company is Arizona's largest electric utility. On a large scale, APS has been researching electric vehicles for at least 25 years and has maintained a fleet of up to 20 electric vehicles during that time. In 1967, APS completed the first cross-country drive of an electric vehicle. The Mars II car travelled from Detroit to Phoenix, 2,226 miles, in 17 days. Today, APS has one of the largest electric vehicle commuter car fleets in the nation.

Its commitment to electric vehicles and research is ongoing. Recently, APS partially funded the purchase of electrically powered buses, for the cities of Phoenix and Glendale, Arizona. They were the second and third cities in the country to purchase a nonpolluting electric bus.

Technological advancements have brought great improvements in the performance of electric vehicles in recent years. California's legislative mandates for cleaner air, as well as the Clean Air Act of 1991, also have prompted dramatic, even feverish, efforts to overcome the technological obstacles that have prevented electric cars from becoming a mass market item. Future advances in technology are expected to make electric cars both practical and affordable.

In fact, recent advancements were showcased in the Inaugural Solar and Electric 500, a contest of speed and endurance for autos powered by batteries or solar rays, held in Phoenix, Arizona in 1991. APS and Southern California Edison co-sponsored the winning electric vehicle, the DEMI Zinc-air battery operated Honda CRX, that set new records for speed and distance.

The biggest advantage of electric vehicles is zero emissions. According to the Electric Power Research Institute, after factoring in power plant emissions for the electricity used to recharge the batteries, electric vehicles are still 90 percent cleaner than internal combustion engines. Electric vehicles do not contribute the unseen pollutants -- carbon monoxide, nitrous oxide and carbon dioxide. In addition, they reduce hazardous wastes since they do not use engine oil or antifreeze. Lead acid batteries used in electric vehicles also are 97 percent recyclable. Electric cars of the future can be one innovation that can help save the earth, while providing convenient and affordable transportation.

Pollution prevention is practiced by APS in the management of the company's conventional vehicles as well. The Transportation and Maintenance Department at APS maintains a fleet of more than 1,500 vehicles from large line trucks to passenger cars. The department recently applied two simple ways to reduce fluorocarbon pollutants in the automotive maintenance area. They now purchase WD-40 lubricant in one-gallon containers and reuse freon in the vehicle's air conditioning system.

Each month, APS mechanics use about three gallons of WD-40, purchased in one-gallon bulk containers. The bulk containers replace the need to purchase 24 WD-40 aerosol spray cans a month, which added fluorocarbons to the environment. The change also eliminates the need to dispose of used aerosol cans. The garage staff pours the bulk lubricant into reusable hand dispensers. These containers don't use aerosol pressure to dispense the product, therefore eliminating the release of fluorocarbons. Converting to bulk containers and reusable dispensers has saved the garage about $30 per month.

Mechanics also are reusing freon when performing maintenance on fleet vehicle air conditioners. Before recharging the car's air conditioner, the mechanics purge the freon into a holding tank, and then run it through a filtering system, preventing the release of fluorocarbon pollutants.

What's in it for APS?

APS's gas-powered fleet has reduced the release of fluorocarbons into the atmosphere, and the use of bulk lubricants has resulted in cost savings. Their extensive research and the use of electric vehicles have positioned the company as a leading expert in existing and pioneering technologies to develop vehicles that reduce auto emissions.

McDonnell Douglas Employees Jump On The Vanwagon

Vanpooling is a convenient way for many McDonnell Douglas employees at four of its sites across the country to commute, and to help clean the air. McDonnell Douglas operates more than 450 vanpools. In the St. Louis, Missouri area alone, nearly 245 vanpools bring 2,500 employees back and forth to work each day. For those employees, some of whom commute nearly 115 miles one way, vanpooling is the only logical alternative to driving alone.

"We pioneered vanpooling at our St. Louis location in 1979," said Greg Lyle, manager of vanpool operations in St. Louis. "There were some government incentive programs that got us interested in trying it, and it really just snowballed. The cost of gas was going up, and people really liked vanpooling."

McDonnell Douglas, a military and commercial aircraft manufacturing company, is the largest defense contractor in the country, and the largest employer in Missouri. Today, nearly 9 percent of the more than 32,000 employees at its approximately one dozen locations in St. Louis participate in the vanpooling program. Nationwide, McDonnell Douglas employees in St. Louis; Tulsa, Oklahoma; Huntington Beach, Long Beach and Santa Anna, California put nearly five million miles on their vans annually.

In St. Louis alone, according to Lyle, vanpooling saves more than 4 million gallons of gas and 50 million commuter miles each year. It also is responsible for reducing the amount of air pollution produced by vehicle emissions.

At its St. Louis location, employees pay all the actual costs of running the vanpools, including gas, maintenance and leasing costs. Costs in St. Louis range from a minimum of $12.50 per week to a maximum of about $34. Costs are contained through a self-insurance policy, competitive maintenance contracts, and a new universal gasoline credit card which streamlines the processing of charges for gas purchases.

Lyle recently spearheaded the design of a "universal gas credit card" that is expected to save McDonnell Douglas $650,000 annually. After talking with the company's vanpool drivers and learning that they used 11 different oil companies in St. Louis alone, Lyle got help from Amoco Oil and the American Petroleum Institute to produce the McDonnell Douglas Van Pool Universal Gas Card. The card will eliminate the use of 7,000 four-part forms and streamline operations.

"Initial $50 cash advances were returned, expense report submittals were changed to monthly (instead of every time a driver needed gas), forms are estimated to drop to approximately 3,000 annually, and our office productivity has increased," said Lyle, summing up the impact of the new approach to keeping van gas tanks full.

What's in it for McDonnell Douglas?

Employees enjoy the savings and personal benefit of having a vanpooling program, and, in their communities, McDonnell Douglas is recognized as a corporation that is concerned about the environment and its employees.

HOW YOUR BUSINESS CAN DO IT, TOO!

POLLUTION & TOXIN ELIMINATION should be a goal of every business. With some ingenuity and resourcefulness businesses can find ways to operate profitably without negatively impacting the environment. To find out what your business can do, first conduct an audit of your business and determine if you can eliminate pollution at the source or prevent toxic substances from entering the environment. Many states with environmental protection agencies also have technical support staff available to assist businesses in developing cost-effective solutions for pollution prevention and toxic waste problems. These services often are free of charge and some states even have grant monies available to businesses who are willing to take measures to eliminate pollution and toxins from their operations.

Whenever possible, purchase products, services, raw materials and supplies for your business that are not damaging to the environment. Be on the lookout for operational activities or materials that cause pollution and ask employees to offer suggestions about how to eliminate any pollution or toxin. If business owners take steps on their own, they may be able to avoid costly and time consuming compliance with new rigid regulations.

Put a ✔ in the box next to the activities you can implement in your daily business operations. Then, list them in the back of the book.

☐ Don't Buy Supplies That Pollute The Environment

Avoid purchasing supplies in aerosol containers. The release of the chlorofluorocarbons in the atmosphere damages the ozone layer. Don't buy styrofoam cups, because they are made from an oil byproduct called benzene which is thought to be carcinogenic and the cups never decompose in the landfill. Use mugs or china cups instead. Purchase cleaning supplies for desks and equipment that are biodegradable and safe for use on all surfaces.

☐ Buy & Use Biodegradable Cleaning Products

Make sure your shop, office, warehouse, workshop or factory is cleaned with products that are not harmful to the environment. Industrial cleaners have been the major source of pollutants in our sewer systems and often are irritating to humans, as well. Today, many new products are available that effectively clean floors, bathrooms and work areas, and they will not pollute the water supply when disposed of in the sewer system. You can save money by using all-purpose cleaners that allow you to buy in bulk, which also reduces packaging. Additional savings can be made by purchasing cleaning concentrates which may cost more up front, but save money in the long run. If you rent your business space, check with the property manager to determine if the cleaning service is using safe products. If not, strongly suggest a switch to cleaning products that will not harm humans or the earth.

☐ Redesign Your Products and Services

If your products and services currently require toxic materials, determine if they can be redesigned to reduce or eliminate the pollution causing substances. Determine if nontoxic materials, such as water-based inks or biodegradable materials, can be substituted.

☐ Modify Your Processing

Look for ways to modify processing to reduce or eliminate the use or generation of pollution and toxins. Explore organic agriculture methods if you raise crops or animals. Use biodegradable detergent and water to clean parts and equipment rather than solvents. Try to recapture and reuse hazardous materials necessary in processing and check out new technologies that can make handling toxins and hazardous materials less detrimental to the environment. Redesign your equipment to accommodate nonpolluting materials and make every attempt to recover waste materials for reuse or resale.

☐ Add Plants To Your Environment

Adding plants to your indoor environment can significantly reduce indoor air pollution, especially in buildings with few windows or windows that do not open. Common office pollutants include formaldehyde from furniture, carpets, wall board and paneling; benzene and trichloroethylene from cigarette smoke, paints, oils, inks and some plastics. Factories and repair shops can experience additional air pollution from processes that emit exhaust. Live, green plants act as air filters and absorb the pollutants through their leaf and root systems. Besides cleaning the air, plants can create a more pleasant workplace. Place one four or five foot plant for every 100 square feet of space and provide a natural solution to eliminating indoor air pollution.

☐ Encourage Employee Ride Sharing and Cut Down Trips In Company Vehicles

Air quality can be significantly improved, especially in areas that have problems with smog, with more careful use of personal and company vehicles. Suggest ways to take cars off the road by encouraging employees to share rides to work and not to make unnecessary trips in company vehicles. Offer discount bus passes or preferential parking for carpoolers. If your employees are concentrated in a certain area, van-pooling may be the answer to attracting loyal employees with this added benefit. While employees still pay the costs of operating the vanpools, the convenience and personal cost-savings are often seen as a real benefit. Why lessen the number of cars on the road? Because in the course of a year, one company car driven 1,000 miles each month can produce almost six tons of carbon dioxide into the atmosphere.

☐ Properly Dispose of Hazardous Waste

If you cannot eliminate all pollution from your man-ufacturing or servicing processes, check with state and local agencies for guidelines on how to properly dispose of hazard-ous waste your company is generating. If all toxins and pollutants cannot be completely eliminated at the source, the next best thing is properly disposing of these wastes.

Chapter 5

Environmentally Safe Products & Services

*"Competition can serve the cause of environmental protection.
Corporate environmentalism can create a competitive edge.
The right thing to do can also be the competitive thing to do."*

Richard J. Mahoney
Chairman and Chief Executive Officer
Monsanto

*"It's a partnership of profits and principles. The company
operates within the world, the environment, the community.
That is where our responsibilities lie -- we want to give
something back to society."*

Anita Roddick
Founder and Managing Director
The Body Shop

*"Never in my career have I seen an issue build faster in its
importance in the consumer's mind than the issue of what
manufacturers are going to do to help the environment."*

John Pepper
President
Proctor & Gamble

*"Our product was developed with the idea that every
consumer can be part of the solution."*
Trisha Hood
Tree Saver, Inc.

Interest in the environment, piqued by the first Earth Day in 1970, was pushed to new heights with the 20th year celebration of Earth Day 1990. Since then, a consumer and marketing frenzy over "going green" has emerged. In fact, more than 11 percent of new products introduced between 1989 and 1990 were making some type of claim to be "green" or environmentally friendly. This seemingly endless number of "green" products has been created to meet the demands of environmentally conscious consumers. "Green" education has been added to our schools' curriculum, and is a prominent message in many media public service and corporate identity campaigns.

Companies that are going "green" today may be seeing gold along the way, but the flood of green products and advertising also has prompted scrutiny by regulators, environmental groups and consumers. Simply labelling a product "environmentally friendly", "biodegradable", or "recyclable" isn't enough, and companies whose products are perceived or found to be harmful to the environment or falsely represented as "green" may see decreased sales and a loss of public trust, as well as possible repercussions from the Federal Trade Commission or their state's attorney general's office.

From a business standpoint, the green movement stands to benefit the economy as well as the earth. Entrepreneurs have found ways to associate products with the environmental movement, everything from shampoo and laundry soap to calendars and t-shirts. Other companies are seizing the opportunity to become involved in environmental issues with public relations programs, such as partnerships with environmental groups, or with marketing promotions such as giving away tree seedlings or touting the new reduced packaging of their products.

Incorporating environmental concerns with a solid business strategy can make a difference and provide a competitive edge. Read on to see what other companies have done.

Earth Care Paper, Inc. Gets A Good Wrap For Recycled Paper Products

Madison, Wisconsin based Earth Care Paper, Inc. is a corporation which specializes in merchandising high quality paper products made from recycled paper. The company has taken many steps in order to offer products which are environmentally safe.

According to Earth Care, manufacturing one ton of paper from waste paper instead of trees will save three cubic yards of landfill space, reduce air pollution by 74 percent and water pollution by 34 percent, use 58 percent less water and 25-75 percent less energy, and will save 17 trees.

The recycled paper products they sell are alternatively bleached; that is, none of the products are bleached with elemental chlorine which creates toxic dioxin pollution. Earth Care also uses soy inks to print its stationery, wrapping papers, cards, and its catalog. The company uses soy bean based inks rather than petroleum inks because petroleum inks contain highly toxic volatile organic compounds (VOC's) that are harmful to people and the environment. Soy inks, which are made from refined soybean oil (the same product used in many cooking oils), reduce the emission of VOC's by up to 80 percent. In addition to being safer, soy ink is a renewable source, whereas petroleum is not.

Earth Care Paper packages their cards, stationery and gift wrap in 100 percent plant fiber cellulose packaging. Cellulose is biodegradable, so it will decompose into harmless compounds. In addition, cellulose is derived from plants which are renewable, so there is no need to worry about a limit on supply.

Earth Care's concern for the environment goes beyond the manufacturing and packaging stage. The company donates 10 percent of its profits to organizations with missions that address environmental and social concerns. Earth Care also includes information on environmental protection in its product catalog.

Since all grades of recycled paper are not manufactured from 100 percent recycled waste, Earth Care contributes funds to tree planting organizations to replace three times the number of trees that were harvested to make the virgin fiber it uses each year.

What's in it for Earth Care?

A market position as a leader of high quality recycled paper products, generating $5.5 million in annual sales.

Tom's of Maine: Pioneering Spirit Pays Off

Maker of natural care products -- toothpaste, deodorant, shampoo, shaving cream, dental floss and mouthwash -- Tom's of Maine is careful to use biodegradable natural ingredients in all its products. Their products contain no preservatives, synthetic colors, animal products or artificial fragrances and they also are tested for safety without using animals. Tom and Kate Chappell established their product standards more than 20 years ago and have stuck to them ever since.

The company's concern for the environment does not stop with the content of its products. Tom's of Maine, one of the first companies to take a stand for environmental protection, makes the only nationally available toothpaste packaged in 100 percent aluminum recyclable tubes. The company is equally careful about being environmentally responsible throughout its manufacturing process and business operations. They make careful purchasing decisions when buying supplies, in addition to their commitment to recycling and conservation.

To reduce water use, the company installed water-saving devices that cut down consumption by one-third -- from 1,200 gallons per day to 800 gallons per day. They also installed a wastewater treatment system which reduces any negative impact on the environment.

Tom's of Maine also practices a comprehensive program of recycling with on-site receptacles that collect office paper, newspaper, corrugated cardboard, aluminum tubes and plastic bottles. Each desk has a personal receptacle for office paper. Other efforts include selling off-spec products as seconds in the company's retail outlet or donating them to nonprofit organizations. Empty fragrance oil drums are donated to the Kennebuck High School to reuse as trash cans. Wooden pallets, 55-gallon drums, chalk bags and obsolete machinery are reused or recycled. The company purchases recycled paper for 96 percent of the office paper supply. Aside from aggressively reducing overall packaging, recycled materials for packaging of the entire product line are being sought; including paperboard, plastic bottles and aluminum materials.

Tom's of Maine donates at least 10 percent of their pretax profits to charity. For example, they developed a partnership with their town planners to develop curbside recycling. Through a $25,000 grant and the use of employee volunteers, the town was able to generate more than 70 percent participation in the recycling program.

What's in it for Tom's of Maine?

Tom's of Maine is a thriving business that caters to the needs of consumers and the environment by providing environmentally safe personal care products. Moreover, sales have increased by 20-25 percent annually over the past five years, while hundreds of thank you letters arrive each week from consumers who appreciate their efforts.

ARCO: Creating Fuel For The Future

In 1989, ARCO introduced to Southern California EC-1 Regular, the nation's first environmentally engineered fuel and the first emission control gasoline. One year later, the company also introduced EC-Premium. These fuels were designed to reduce environmentally damaging emissions and to produce air quality benefits much faster and less expensively than other alternatives. And, that's exactly what they did.

As a matter of fact, over the past two years, use of ARCO's EC-1 Regular and EC-Premium have resulted in a reduction of more than 150 million pounds of pollutants from California's skies.

Independently conducted tests show that vehicles using ARCO EC-1 Regular gasoline emit fewer of the reactive chemical components that are precursors of smog, such as nitrogen oxides and organic gases. Vehicles using this fuel also give off less carbon monoxide than those using conventional gasoline. Plus, fewer pollutants are produced without diminished engine performance or the need for costly new equipment or engine retrofits.

EC-1 Regular is especially designed for older cars and trucks without catalytic converters. EC-Premium is a superior grade gasoline, environmentally engineered to provide immediate air quality benefits to Southern California. EC-Premium has an exceptionally low benzene content - - 63 percent below the average for all premium gasoline in the Los Angeles area.

This dramatic reduction in benzene content was achieved through refinery processing changes that lower the total amount of benzene produced by as much as 12,600 gallons a day. Independently conducted tests demonstrate that EC-Premium generates 28 percent less carbon monoxide and 21 percent less hydrocarbon emissions than the average unreformulated premium gasoline. These reductions translate into an 86,000 pound reduction of motor vehicle pollutants into the Los Angeles Basin air -- every day!

During the summer of 1991, ARCO announced the development of an environmentally superior formula (EC- X) that will reduce gasoline's smog-producing potential by at least 37 percent and toxic emissions by at least 47 percent. The fuel also will reduce late-model vehicle emissions to levels no greater than those generated by state-of-the-art flexible fuel vehicles using themethanol fuel, M85.

While EC-X is designed for outstanding driving performance, it shows reductions of 28 percent in hydrocarbon tailpipe emissions, 36 percent in evaporative emissions and 26 percent in nitrogen oxide emissions -- the three main ingredients in smog. If EC-X was used by all cars and trucks in California, the state's vehicular emissions would be reduced by an average of 3.8 million pounds or 1,900 tons per day. That's the equivalent of taking eight million vehicles -- almost a third of the registered cars and trucks -- off California's roads every day!

What's in it for ARCO?

ARCO has managed to hold 20 percent of the West Coast's gasoline market and has made a significant contribution to reducing air pollution in Southern California.

Tree Free - The Real Thing

The Tree-Free Co., a privately-owned company located in Augusta, Maine, manufactures all of its paper products from 100 percent recycled paper. Since 1973, it has recycled more than 2.7 billion pounds of wastepaper that otherwise would have gone to landfills.

The company began selling its paper towels, napkins, facial tissues and bathroom tissues in 1990. In late 1991, it introduced two new cleaning products, a glass cleaner and an all-purpose cleaner. The cleaners are hypoallergenic and use safe, natural enzyme formulas to biodegrade the stain and odor causing substances.

Tree-Free has gained recognition for using 100 percent de-inked recycled paper for its products, and also for its efforts in source reduction, space conservation and fuel conservation. In 1990 and 1991, Tree-Free was commended by Earth Day New York City for manufacturing all of its products from 100 percent recycled paper and for its leadership position as a company that is sensitive to the environment.

"We are genuinely concerned about the environment," said Brian Ingalls, general manager. "We realize we still have a way to go, and will continue to develop and introduce products that are ecologically responsible."

What's in it for Tree-Free?

A substantial business and recognition as the only consumer products paper company in the United States that manufactures all of its products from 100 percent recycled paper.

E-TECH: Special Pumps Provide Heating And Cooling

In Anaheim, California this company is distributing and installing a specialty air-to-water heat pump with new technology that provides both heating and cooling. It is an ideal solution for many commercial facilities that rely on gas boilers to heat large quantities of water, such as hotels, kitchens and restaurants. The unit provides hot water while cooling the air, and since it is an all-electric unit with no combustion involved, there is no concern about meeting pollution abatement guidelines that require reductions in nitrogen oxide emissions from natural gas boilers.

The Heat Pump Water Heaters (HPWH) work much like air conditioners, removing heat from the environment and returning cooler, drier air. But in this case, the heat is used to raise water temperature rather than simply being rejected outdoors. HPWH's are able to heat water more efficiently than natural gas because they transfer heat rather than produce it. They also deliver space cooling and dehumidification as byproducts.

Several types of businesses can simultaneously make use of both the hot and cold sides of an HPWH. A restaurant kitchen is ideal. When a heat pump is used to heat the water for cleaning and washing, it can provide cool air directly into the kitchen. It either supplements the existing air conditioning system, thereby reducing electrical consumption, or provides comfort to employees who previously worked in a very hot environment.

Locker rooms of spas or health clubs also can take maximum advantage of the benefits of a HPWH. As water for the showers is being heated, cool dry air from the evaporator can be discharged into the locker room, providing greater comfort for a lesser cost than conventional heating and cooling systems. Laundromats and indoor municipal swimming pools also adapt well to this technology.

The typical payback time for heat pump water heating is less than 3 years, and using a heat pump leads to a fifty percent reduction in energy consumption. When used to replace electric water heaters, water heating costs are reduced by more than fifty percent.

"One of the major hurdles facing the HPWH is the lack of customer awareness and the perceived notion that gas is the most economical and efficient form of water heating," said Vasant K. Agarwal, CEO of E-Tech. "We've done thousands of installations across the country over the past 10 years, and the HPWH has proven to be an attractive alternative technology."

What's in it for E-Tech?

E-TECH enjoys $2.5 million in annual sales, and has satisfied customers who have realized substantial savings on their energy bills.

The Body Shop Knows What's Good For A Body

The Body Shop, which Anita Roddick began in the United Kingdom as a tiny shop in 1976, is a rapidly expanding, international business which specializes in "naturally based" lotions and potions for the body. There are now more than 700 stores in nearly 40 countries, including 78 in the United States.

The Body Shop prides itself on selling only environmentally safe products that are made, whenever possible, from close-to-source vegetable rather than animal ingredients. Those ingredients, and the final products, are not tested on animals. In addition to offering environmentally safe, biodegradable products, The Body Shop encourages recycling by providing many of its products in refillable containers and offering its customers discounts when those containers are returned for subsequent purchases.

Its sales approach also is different from other companies in the cosmetics industry. The company associates its products with health and well-being, rather than selling hype and fantasies. It refrains from advertising its products, and instead focuses its efforts on providing clear, factual and honest information about the product and its ingredients on the labels and to customers in their stores.

Many of the ingredients, in fact, are found during Ms. Roddick's frequent trips to remote areas of Third World countries. She talks with the local people about their hair and skin care regimens, and incorporates the information and ideas into her products and stores.

Concern for the environment doesn't stop with the contents of products made by The Body Shop or their manufacturing process. The company, which expresses its concerns for global environmental issues to its employees and customers, is known for activism on many causes ranging from saving the rain forest to saving the whales.

The Body Shop is known for its truly unique product line -- one that is responsible to the environment in many different ways.

What's in it for The Body Shop?

Pretax profits of $23 million on sales of $141 million at the end of 1990, and an average 50 percent growth each year during the last decade.

ECOVER Uncovers Safe Products

ECOVER was started in 1979 in Belgium by Frans Boggaerts. Armed with more than 20 years experience in the detergent industry, he created a line of alternative products which would work as effectively as commercial cleaners but have as little negative environmental impact as possible.

Today, the ECOVER product line includes fabric softener, laundry washing powders and liquids, a wool wash liquid, nonchlorine bleach, cream cleanser, floor soap, toilet cleaner and dishwashing liquid. Their products are manufactured in Belgium and the U.S. and sold in more than 30 countries. ECOVER products are made without the use of phosphates, enzymes, optical brighteners, chlorine bleaches, petroleum based detergents, NTA, EDTA and synthetic perfumes or colorings. Their products are not tested on animals.

To educate consumers and promote their products, ECOVER has produced "The ECOVER Code" as a guideline to help consumers understand many of the manufacturing processes and ingredients that are part of conventional cleaning products and why use of those products can have a strong negative impact on the eco-system.

"At ECOVER, we feel a strong responsibility to do our part in preserving the planet," said Ellen Weiser, ECOVER spokesperson.

What's in it for ECOVER?

ECOVER has built a successful, profitable international business providing effective, environmentally responsible household products. Educating the public about the impact of consumer products on the environment has been a successful component of the company's marketing strategy.

HOW YOUR BUSINESS CAN DO IT, TOO!

ENVIRONMENTALLY SAFE PRODUCTS AND SERVICES are a key ingredient to any company's plan for saving the earth. Producing and using such products goes hand-in-hand with eliminating pollutants and toxins from our environment. Prompted by increased attention to environmental concerns, more companies are creating new products or modifying existing ones to be less harmful to the environment. Environmental concerns of business owners and managers are receiving greater attention because consumers and customers are demanding "earth safe" products and services.

Thus, the "green" movement can signal opportunities for your company to develop a new product or service to meet these consumer demands, or to gain a competitive edge. The trend also is expected to produce a wider choice of alternative products that you can use at your business, as well. As more consumers opt to spend their dollars with companies that are environmentally responsible, business owners and managers will realize that business survival and success can depend on how the public views their relationship with the earth.

Put a ✔ in the box next to the activities that you can implement in your daily business operations. Then, list them in the back of the book.

☐ Research The Alternatives

Are there better ways to manufacture your products so they have a minimal impact on the environment? Enlist the help of local or industry experts to review your processing and seek ways to eliminate any harmful ingredients. Modify your operations to reduce or eliminate processing steps that damage the earth. Many trade associations can provide a wealth of information on current research and/or new, safer supplies. When positive changes have been made, announce them to the news media.

☐ Get Creative

Many new products and services have been introduced in response to concerns about the environment. Perhaps there is a market niche which your company can fill with a new product, or a new way to promote existing safe products. Remember, though, simply tacking on a "green" label will not give your product instant acceptance. Products truly must be safe for the environment; otherwise, customers lose trust in companies that make false claims.

☐ Create Recycled Products

Whenever possible, use recycled materials to create new or existing products. In addition, show your concern for the environment by purchasing supplies and goods from other companies whose products are made from recycled resources. The increased demand for recycled products will create greater demand for recyclable materials, thus helping build the market for both materials and products. When materials that can be recycled are in greater demand, people will have a stronger incentive to increase their recycling efforts.

☐ Provide Clean Up And "Know How" Services

Many new companies are emerging to deal with environmental problems or with the protection of the earth. For example, companies that specialize in hazardous waste management or provide consulting services to assure compliance with environmental regulations are apt to be growth companies of the future. If your company has expertise in a specific area of environmental protection, consider packaging and selling the service to others in your industry.

☐ Communicating Environmental Information

Business owners, managers and consumers are interested in obtaining information about the environment and how to protect the earth. Determine if your company can capitalize on the demand for information by packaging and selling your environmental expertise.

Chapter 6

Waste Management Control

"Our customers are becoming increasingly sensitive to the amount and type of packaging in their purchases."

Keith Tice
National Director for Packaging & Labeling
Sears Merchandise Group
Sears Roebuck & Company

"Recycling is an idea whose time has come. Accompanying the recycling boom are many opportunities for entrepreneurs to produce products from scrap materials."

Glenn Wallace
Manager, Resource Recovery
3M

"Recycling will be a permanent part of how we manage our waste in this country. At BFI, we made a corporate commitment to be a leader in recycling. Working together, we can leave a better, cleaner world for the future."

William D. Ruckelhaus
Chairman and CEO
Browning-Ferris Industries

Until recent years, American business owners and consumers in our disposable, throwaway society gave little thought to what happened to their trash after it was hauled away. Now they are concerned, and rightly so. According to estimates from the Environmental Protection Agency (EPA), nearly half of all landfills could be closed by 1995. It's getting harder to find a place to stash the trash, since nobody wants a landfill in their backyard. In addition, hauling and disposal costs are increasing, and so is the tax burden required to handle the problem.

The shortage of landfill space poses a major problem for municipalities and businesses. The vast majority of trash from consumers and households, as much as 80 percent, is buried in landfills. Only half of the remainder is recycled, and the final 10 percent is incinerated.

The EPA has calculated that each American produces an average of more than three pounds of trash per day, totalling up to 160 million tons of solid municipal waste annually. Packaging accounts for half of the volume, and that's just from consumers. The total amount of waste created by industry, manufacturing, business and agriculture is even higher.

Hazardous and toxic waste generated by business and industry pose special problems for the environment, since they can pollute and destroy our water supply, impact air quality and damage the soil. Responsible management of these wastes is essential to protect the earth.

Businesses have taken steps to curb or prevent waste, both in their facilities and their consumer products. Trash hauling expenses and tipping fees, regulations on hazardous waste disposal, and other associated costs provide the economic incentives to reduce and manage waste. On the market side, environmentally conscious consumers are demanding that business and industry offer products with less packaging.

Effective waste management can save your company money while promoting good will among your customers. Here are several examples of how other companies have handled the waste management issue.

Kinnear Door Employees Provide Simple Solution To Waste Management Dilemma

Kinnear Door employees found a simple, economical and safe solution to handling the company's wastewater disposal problem. The company, located in Centralia, Washington, is part of the Wayne-Dalton Corporation located in Mount Hope, Ohio. It manufactures wooden sections for overhead garage doors. It employs up to 100 workers at the Washington location, and 13 to 14 million board feet of lumber goes through the plant each year.

Its manufacturing processes include drying, milling, jointing and gluing wood sections to form door panels and other building products. New infrared ovens provide fast, energy-efficient drying of glued sections. A septic system, installed when the plant was built in 1963, was initially used to dispose of wastewater which contained mostly glue wash-down water. Later, environmental regulations called for the company to store waste water so that a septic pumper could take it to be sprayed at a nearby landfill. Changes in landfill regulations, though, eliminated this option and created quite a dilemma for Kinnear Door on how to dispose of the 2,500 gallons of wastewater it generated each month.

They worked on solutions for more than a year, evaluating options such as settling ponds, evaporators and pretreatment with transportation to a local sewage treatment plant. The most promising alternative, pretreatment, would require environmental permit procedures and would cost $10,000 a year for testing and caustic pretreatment chemicals. Both workers and management were reluctant to bring another hazardous chemical into the plant.

The final solution came from Kinnear's own employees. "The idea started with the people who were involved in the actual operation and knew the processes the best. Everyone got involved," said John Ver Valen, a purchasing agent for Kinnear Door.

The solution was to reuse the glue wash-down water when mixing up the glue formulations. The glues were water-based, so the company switched to powdered products which could be mixed with washwater instead of freshwater. The glue companies tested various blends of wastewater and powdered glue to ensure high product quality.

The entire program required only two barrels, pumps and a fiberglass settling tank to collect and hold the wastewater. The investment was minimal, the payoff great.

What's in it for Kinnear Door?

For just $1,500, and with the ingenuity of its employees, Kinnear Door was able to save $1,000 a year in annual permit fees, $300 a month in sewer fees and an estimated $10,000 per year in pretreatment costs. Landfill disposal costs also were reduced, and the problems of storing and handling hazardous chemicals were avoided.

Eastman Kodak: Reducing Waste At Its Source

From the very beginning, Eastman Kodak has made many attempts to reduce waste. They have managed to recover 100 percent of the waste fiber used in the production of their photographic paper, of which 25 percent is recycled and used in paper production. In addition, the company has undertaken new production methods which reduce waste in film manufacturing. Over the past five years, waste from the production of raw film rolls has been reduced by 47 percent and, by means of quality film finishing programs, waste from cutting and trimming 35mm and disk film has been reduced by 29 percent over the last three years.

More than 355,000 pounds of paperboard is saved annually through a reduction-at-the-source measure taken by Kodak's Consumer Imaging Division. Photo processing chemicals are shipped to customer labs in single cartons with dividers, rather than in several, separate containers.

Packaging for color negative paper shipments to photofinishing labs has been redesigned to reduce the amount of corrugated containerboard used. The same amount of product is still delivered, but 192,000 pounds less containerboard is used per year.

Kodak's waste reduction program is working at other company divisions as well. Kodak installed special process controls and devices at its Sterling Drug, Inc. pharmaceutical manufacturing facility in Barceloneta, Puerto Rico. This effort has led to a more than 300 percent increase in production, with no increase in the amount of solvent waste.

What's the bottom line for Eastman Kodak?

Kodak's waste reduction program has eliminated tons of refuse from ending up in landfills and has saved the company tens of millions of dollars.

Saddleback Homes: On-Site Construction Recycling

Saddleback Homes, a home builder in Scottsdale, Arizona, started an experimental recycling program for construction waste, perhaps the first of its kind in the nation.

Larry Kush, president of Saddleback Homes, felt that materials such as wood, plastic, cardboard, wire and metal could be recycled in designated bins on the lot as the homes are being built. Once the materials have been gathered in special four-part bins, they are hauled to various facilities for recycling.

"It is estimated that more than 20 percent of all landfill space consists of general construction waste," said Kush. "Those in the construction industry should begin taking a more responsible role in solving this environmental problem. If our program is successful, we hope other home builders and commercial construction businesses will learn from this experiment and look into the recycling of construction waste materials."

The only problem they have faced is a lack of facilities for recycling building materials such as gypsum and masonry. With the help of a company called "Why Waste America," wood is recycled into paper pulp and wafer board. A method for recycling gypsum and masonry is currently being researched. They are confident, however, that in working with the Commission on the Arizona Environment and various Arizona recycling facilities, they can solve some of the logistical problems in the disposal of construction waste.

The results of their recycling efforts have been nothing but positive. Due to favorable press exposure, one new home buyer chose to have their family house built by Saddleback Homes directly because of the recycling program.

The first house to be built using the waste recycling process was that of Jeffery and Cherece Griswold. Griswold, an environmental science high school teacher for the Paradise Valley school district, is delighted that his home was the first to be involved with the on-site construction waste recycling effort. "By recycling at the source, Saddleback Homes is not only eliminating the visual eyesore usually associated with construction sites, but also demonstrating environmental responsibility, uncharacteristic of the industry," he said.

What's in it for Saddleback Homes?

In addition to doing something positive for the environment, Saddleback Homes has enjoyed lots of positive publicity from the local media and, as a result, new homes sales.

First Brands: First Class Environmental Commitment

First Brands, based in Danbury, Connecticut, practices environmental commitment in far-reaching ways. Over the past several years the company, which makes GLAD Wrap and Bags, and PRESTONE, STP and SIMONIZ brand automotive products, has emphasized environmentally responsible manufacturing policies.

In the area of waste reduction, First Brands has downgauged the plastic used in GLAD brand waste disposal bags while maintaining the product's strength and quality. This initiative saves more than 20 million pounds of plastic each year.

The company also operates an extensive in-plant recycling program, in which 50 million pounds of plastic trimmings and scrap paper are reclaimed per year. Recycled (preconsumer) paperboard also is used for the retail packaging of GLAD Wrap and Bag products, saving hundreds of thousands of trees.

First Brands' efforts in other areas include the elimination of toxic inks, downgauging of plastic packaging where possible, use of postconsumer resin in some plastic bottles, downsizing of products so less packaging material is required, and the use of recycled (preconsumer) paperboard for packaging.

What's in it for First Brands?

Its many efforts at waste reduction save the company millions of dollars annually and alleviate pressure on the landfill.

Hyatt: Introducing A New Environmental Awareness

In June 1991, Chicago-based Hyatt hotels and resorts introduced a new environmental awareness and recycling program which reduces by 30 percent the amount of Hyatt garbage sent to landfills.

Cited as the most extensive program in the lodging industry, the new plan involves all 55,000 Hyatt employees and calls for implementation of recycling programs at all 159 hotels. Thirty percent of the Hyatt hotels already have recycling programs in place. In fact, since 1982 the majority of Hyatt hotels have been using napkins, hand towels, stationery, envelopes and tissue made from recycled products.

In accordance with the new plan, programs to recycle cardboard, newspaper and, where possible, other items such as glass, aluminum and soap, will be implemented at all Hyatt hotels in the U.S., Canada and the Carribean by 1992.

Research estimates that the typical Hyatt guest room generates 383 pounds of garbage each year. Under the new plan, rooms will generate an average of only 36.5 pounds of nonrecyclable garbage annually.

What's in it for Hyatt?

Energy savings, less waste sent to the landfill and annual corporate savings of $3 million.

TAMCO Benefits From Tougher Government Regulations

TAMCO, located in San Bernadino County, is a steel mini-mill, the only one of its kind in California. It produces steel reinforcing bars for the construction industry, and is one of the few companies whose increased production means that more waste is removed from the environment and recycled.

TAMCO's primary raw material is waste ferrous scrap metal, material that otherwise would be deposited in a landfill, in fields or along the roadside. Through its recycling efforts, TAMCO used approximately 400,000 tons of waste ferrous scrap metal in 1991.

Recycling is critical to TAMCO's operation. Other companies and municipalities have found that TAMCO's process is an attractive alternative to dumping in landfills, especially since government regulations have called for California cities and counties to reduce their reliance on solid waste landfills by 25 percent in 1995 and 50 percent by the year 2000.

In another area of waste management, TAMCO is working with a local oil recycling firm and the California Department of Health Services to manage used oil filters. It is estimated that at least 22 million used oil filters were targeted for California landfills last year. Through this program, the oil recycler collects, decontaminates, and crushes the used filters. It recovers approximately two million gallons of recyclable oil annually, and TAMCO recycles the remaining scrap metal -- 878,000 pounds of used oil filters in 1991 -- diverting a sizable amount of hazardous or solid waste from landfills.

What's in it for TAMCO?

Its waste management efforts and use of recycled scrap metal in the production of its products save precious landfill space and generate substantial revenues for the company.

Reynolds: Trimming Packaging To Reduce Waste

Reynolds Metals Company, the world's largest producer of aluminum foil and one of the largest makers of aluminum beverage cans, is committed to minimizing the effects their products have on the nation's municipal solid waste stream. Reynolds has proven that source materials can be decreased within existing product parameters in order to reduce waste and still satisfactorily meet consumer needs.

Reynolds has managed to reduce the size and the amount of bulk in their products. For instance, the size of aluminum beverage cans has been reduced by shortening the end of the can and using thinner amounts of aluminum for the actual body stock. Reynolds invented the modern two-piece, drawn-and-ironed aluminum can which now weighs less than 26 pounds per thousand versus the earliest cans which weighed 48 pounds per thousand.

The Reynolds program of converting from solvent-based to water-based inks, coatings and adhesives has been hailed by regulatory officials as an example of an innovative, progressive way to deal with a major environmental challenge. Today, over 75 percent of the production in the company's Bellwood printing plant uses water-based products.

Another attempt Reynolds has made towards waste management control is through the production of packages used to hold its products. Cartons are now made out of recycled paperboard so they may be recycled along with the products they contain.

What's in it for Reynolds Metals Company?

The change to water-based ink has saved Reynolds $30 million and the reduction of raw materials in its aluminum products also saves money and reduces the amount of waste that might go to the landfill when aluminum is not properly recycled.

Spencer USA, Inc. Equipment Collects Hazardous Waste For Safer Disposal

Spencer USA, a drycleaning supplier located in Scottsdale, Arizona, has developed an industrial drycleaning machine that safely uses perchloroethylene, or perc, a hazardous substance regulated by the Environmental Protection Agency. The machine, known as the Universal Mammoth, has a 380-pound dry weight capacity. It is being marketed to replace traditional laundry equipment used by cleaners who do large volumes of grease and oil stained garments.

Its closed, dry-to-dry system provides a more economical alternative to other methods of drycleaning and prevents solvents from entering the environment. It is said to reclaim more than 90 percent of the solvent used in the drycleaning process. The garments are loaded into the tumbler and the solvent is added and circulated. The solvent is then drawn off into the still, where it is vaporized. That vaporizing process "wrings out" the solvent and any leftover material is cooked into a tar-like substance that can be reclaimed and properly disposed.

Next, the garments are heated in the wheel and the solvent is removed and cooled down. A sensor tests for the presence of perc. Fresh air is circulated and the solvent is passed through a charcoal bed, where it is dehydrated. Then the garments are cooled down and the sensor makes one last check for perc. The process prevents large quantities of hazardous materials from entering the environment.

Other industries also have found the process useful. Mining companies have used it to get the perc out of ore and other companies have used it to rid laboratory equipment of grease.

What's in it for Spencer USA?

Through this technology, Spencer USA has enabled drycleaners to minimize their costs, while safely using an effective cleaning solvent without causing damage to the environment. Also, drycleaners using the equipment can clean more garments per hour than those using traditional dry cleaning equipment, reducing expenses while making their operation one-third more efficient.

Burger King Lean Packaging Nets Whopping Savings

Burger King, a fast-food restaurant chain headquartered in Miami, Florida, is dedicated to waste reduction. Since its founding in 1954, the corporation has been using principally paper packaging for its products, but in July 1991, it enhanced that effort.

Burger King has begun switching all of its sandwich packaging from paperboard cartons to paper wrap in each of its 6,500 restaurants worldwide. This change is expected to save about 15,000 tons of paper per year. It also will reduce by about a four to one ratio the number of corrugated cartons used to ship the wrappers to the restaurants. These two changes will mean far less product to ship, resulting in fewer deliveries, less gas used and fewer vehicle emissions into the atmosphere.

Burger King also has begun using new "Good News" white paper bags for takeout orders. These bags are made from recycled newspapers with an overall recycled content of 65 percent. It is expected that more than 8,000 tons of newspapers per year will be recycled into Burger King's "Good News" bags.

In addition, Burger King is actively supporting research by the Michigan Biotechnological Institute in the mass application of composting, and is developing a pilot program in the Minneapolis area to turn waste into compost.

"It's fantastic that Burger King Corporation has taken the initiative to do something that's beneficial to the environment, the customer and the businessman," said Dennis Hitzeman, a Burger King franchisee in Phoenix, Arizona. "Burger King's efforts are resulting in less pollution for the environment, easier handling for the customer, and cost savings for the franchisee. Everybody wins!"

The corporation's concern for the environment does not stop with solid waste management. Since 1987, Burger King has had a policy of not purchasing beef from any countries that raise cattle on what was once tropical rain forest land. Their beef today comes almost exclusively from United States suppliers who buy their beef primarily from the United States, Canada, Australia, New Zealand and Ireland.

What's in it for Burger King?

Savings result from the annual reduction of at least 15,000 tons of paper packaging that won't get into the landfills. Also, the reduction in packaging translates into consumer and activist appreciation, as well as bottom line savings.

Cloquet Radiator Repair

With the help of the Minnesota Office of Waste Management, Cloquet Radiator Repair in Cloquet, Minnesota, has found an economical and safe way to manage disposal and reuse of the caustic solutions used to clean out radiator sections before they are resoldered.

In the process of cleaning or "boiling out" radiator sections, the caustic solutions become contaminated with dirt, rust and other debris as well as lead, copper, zinc and tin. These contaminants adversely affect the cleaning capability of the ultrasonic washer. After being used to clean a radiator, the solution is cooled to allow the precipitates to settle. About 80 percent of the solution can then be recycled.

Cloquet devised a system to recover metals from the remaining sludge for recycling, return the additional usable caustic solution to its boil-out tank, and allow the clarified liquid to be safely and legally sewered.

After the original clarified solution is returned to the tank, the remaining liquified sludge is left to settle for another week or two. Any remaining liquid is then pumped into the boil-out tank, and the leftover sludge portion is mixed with sodium sulfide and allowed to settle once again. The heavy metals precipitate out as sulfides.

The liquid from this process, which is nearly 75 percent of the total volume, contains less than 1 part per million lead and can be safely sewered in some communities. The remaining precipitate is mixed with peat moss to form a heavy paste which dries over several days. This paste is then suitable for a secondary lead smelter or a licensed hazardous waste disposal facility. The total cost for a small radiator repair shop to construct this system is approximately $550.

This innovative process was developed through a grant program administered by the Minnesota Office of Waste Management (MOWM). MOWM seeks out problem waste streams and environmentally insensitive industrial processes where prevention and reduction technologies do not exist. It funds efforts to develop new methods and technologies to address the problem. The grant program does not fund existing, vendor available technology; rather, it helps develop new technologies to help industry get out of the regulatory loop. MOWM offers a full report and manual which lets any radiator shop implement the system for themselves. The report can be obtained by contacting MOWM, listed in the resource section later in this book.

What's in it for Cloquet?

Safely disposing of hazardous waste and recovery of recyclable resources lets Cloquet Radiator Repair save money and avoid fines and penalties.

Sears Enlists Suppliers In Waste Reduction Campaign

Sears, Roebuck and Co., headquartered in Chicago, Illinois, has formed a partnership with 2,300 of its suppliers to reduce by 25 percent the amount of packaging used for its merchandise by the end of 1994. Sears and its partners intend to achieve this goal through two methods: by cutting the amount of product packaging used and by increasing the use of recycled materials in the packaging of merchandise.

"We believe our new environmental partnership is significant because it is an integrated and comprehensive program, linking thousands of American companies with Sears in a broad-based commitment to address the country's solid waste disposal problem," said Laurence E. Cudmore, president of retail for Sears Merchandising Group.

Sears has asked its suppliers to find practical and innovative ways to reduce the amount of solid waste by eliminating packaging wherever possible and by increasing the use of recycled paper and plastic for future product packaging. Sears has set four major objectives and deadlines for the program:

* Reduce by at least 10 percent the volume and weight of a product's packaging material by the end of 1992.

* Increase the level of recycled materials in corrugated containers to 25 percent by the end of 1992.

* Increase the use of recycled materials in plastic containers to 20 percent by the end of 1995.

* Utilize the highest recycled content materials possible in other types of packaging, such as folding cartons.

The environmental partnership has already produced some results. A change to no plastic packaging of individual screwdrivers and pliers manufactured by Western Forge Corp., which makes Sears Craftsman hand tools, will eliminate about 78 tons of plastic annually. Whirlpool estimates that it will eliminate 553 tons of packaging materials from boxes for Kenmore dishwashers, refrigerators, and clothes dryers in 1992.

What's in it for Sears?

Sears estimates the program will annually reduce about 1.5 million tons of packaging by the end of 1994 and save the company about $5 million per year, beginning in 1992.

L'eggs Cracks Open New Packaging Design

Two decades ago, an innovative package design helped to bring fame and national name recognition to the L'eggs hosiery line, a division of Sara Lee Corporation which is located in Winston-Salem, North Carolina. The familiar plastic egg-shaped containers made a successful launch into supermarkets, drug stores and mass merchandise stores across the country, bringing women a new source for high quality, name brand hosiery.

In 1991, that familiar plastic egg hatched into a new, single-piece cardboard package. The new package features style, size and shade information that is easier for consumers to understand, and is better for the environment as well.

The new cardboard box uses 38 percent less material and is made from recycled paper. While the familiar plastic egg container also was recyclable, the new package will be easier to handle and more packages will fit into a given display space in the stores. The package will be a single-piece paperboard carton that features L'eggs signature egg shape in silhouette form.

"Our customers tell us that, as much as they have enjoyed the plastic egg container over the years, they are with us all the way in this change," said Ronald W. Zabel, president of L'eggs Product, Inc. Research showed that consumers prefer the new package to the plastic egg by a 2-1 ratio, citing ease of handling and environmental benefits as key reasons for their preferences.

What's in it for L'eggs?

Their new, user-friendly package contains 38 percent less materials and is designed to fit more product on the store shelves. More importantly, the package demonstrates the company's sensitivity to customers' preferences for more contemporary, easy-to-shop packaging and their own corporate environmental concerns about reducing waste at the source.

HOW YOUR BUSINESS CAN DO IT, TOO!

WASTE MANAGEMENT CONTROL can have beneficial results for your business as well as the environment. By reducing packaging your company can save money. By decreasing the amount of waste generated by your company you can save on landfill disposal costs. The proper disposal of wastes, both hazardous and non-hazardous, also is a good business practice. Doing so prevents costly fines, as well as detrimental publicity that could result if your business is found to be not complying with regulations.

By investigating your manufacturing process or service operations you may find your waste materials could be reused by another company for another purpose. Exchanging waste materials is a great way to help the environment, network with another business, and save you money. There are other ways to manage your company's waste and make wise purchasing decisions that can help save the earth and money, too.

Put a ✔ in the box next to the activities you can implement in your daily business operations. Then, list them in the back of the book.

☐ Buy In Bulk

Check with all your vendors to determine if you can buy items in bulk or without excess packaging.

☐ Buy Quality

When purchasing new equipment, make sure it is well-built and can be easily and economically maintained. It is better to spend a little more money on a quality piece of equipment that can provide years of service than to spend less on equipment that may need replacement much sooner. Before you discard your old equipment determine if you can either sell it or give it to someone who can refurbish it for use or resale.

☐ Break The Coffee Cup Break

Discourage the use of nonbiodegradable plastic or styrofoam cups by giving every employee a ceramic coffee mug. Provide spoons instead of plastic stirrers -- and, of course, a place to wash the cups and utensils.

☐ Avoid Disposables

Purchase disposable items only as a last resort. Try to purchase items that can be reused over and over. Use washable plastic or china dinnerware and silverware in the employee cafeteria. Purchase office supplies that can be refilled or reused, such as printer toner cartridges.

☐ Buy Paper Padded Mailer Bags

Mail bags that are padded with a paper product filling can be recycled and offer as much protection as the mailing envelopes filled with plastic bubble linings.

☐ Reduce Junk Mail

Ask employees to place any duplicate mailings or unsolicited junk mail in a collection box. The volume may surprise you. Then, on a periodic basis, assign an employee to send a postcard to solicitors and ask that your company be taken off their routine bulk mailing lists. Contact the Direct Marketing Association in New York for further assistance in getting your company name off the junk mail rosters.

☐ Check It Out

Review all your manufacturing and purchasing procedures to find ways in which you can reduce waste. Reducing waste at the source saves money on the initial purchase as well as in landfill fees.

☐ Change To Cloth Towel Dispensers

Using towel dispensers with reusable cloth towel rolls instead of paper towels reduces waste, keeps your restrooms free of towel litter, and makes bathroom cleanup more efficient.

☐ Use Reusable Forced Air Filters

Installing reusable stainless steel air conditioning and furnace filters can save your company money while reducing waste.

☐ Trade-offs

Investigate local or regional waste exchanges. Often one company's trash can become a useful commodity or raw material for another business. It's a good way to avoid landfill and disposal costs for your waste materials while at the same time helping another company save the earth by reusing otherwise discarded materials.

☐ Donate Used Goods

Rather than adding more to the landfills, donate used equipment or furniture to local charities or other nonprofit organizations. Your throw away items may still be of value to another group.

☐ Check With The Experts

There may be ways to improve your manufacturing processes by reusing water, recapturing wastes for reuse, or even converting the waste to energy. Your local state or municipal government often can provide technical assistance, at no cost or for a nominal charge. There may even be grant money available to help you get started.

☐ Plastic or Cardboard Pallets

Replacing wooden pallets with lighter plastic or cardboard pallets can decrease transportation costs while providing longer use, depending upon your business needs.

☐ Get Your Customers and Employees Involved

Your employees might have great ideas on how to improve your packaging or manufacturing processes to produce less waste. Customers also can be encouraged to return reusable items, such as wire hangers from a dry cleaner.

☐ Reduce Your Packaging

You'll save money if you can implement ways to reduce your packaging and still protect your products and give them the right image.

Chapter 7

Preservation of Natural Resources & Wildlife

"The rain forests will survive only if we add value to them by encouraging their productive use rather than their destruction."

Richard Ruch
Chief Executive Officer
Herman Miller

"Our policy will have a dramatic and immediate effect on saving dolphin lives."

Dr. A. J. F. O'Reilly
Chairman, President & CEO
H.J. Heinz Company

"Our family was raised on the land, and we have a healthy respect for it. People are finally beginning to realize that it's important to give something back to the earth. That's the best way to get quality out."

James Fetzer
President
Fetzer Vineyards

As we tend to our businesses, concern for the rain forests and the creatures in our oceans may be far from our minds. After all, the rain forests are thousands of miles away. Yet, we have come to learn the world's ecosystem, with all its plants, animals and natural resources, is interdependent and must become everyone's concern if we are to preserve life as we know it. Humans no longer can treat the earth as a dumping ground for all mankind's trash, nor rob it of all its treasures. We realize that what happens in the oceans or rain forests can have a profound impact on our lifestyle, economic well-being and very existence.

Although tropical rain forests cover only about seven percent of the land on earth, they are home to at least 66 percent of all plant and animal species. They also provide many products including timber, fruits, spices, nuts, vegetables, medicines and industrial materials like oils, rubber and waxes. In addition, tropical rain forests moderate the earth's air temperature, and play a crucial role in the hydrologic cycle as they absorb rainfall and release moisture.

These rain forests, rich in raw materials, have been cleared for logging, farming, cattle ranching and development to meet the needs for jobs, farms and home sites of people in many Third World countries where the rain forests are found. The widespread deforestation, while meeting some immediate economic and practical needs and satisfying a previously un-checked demand for tropical woods and other products, has lead to fuel wood shortages, soil erosion, climate changes and flooding. It also has caused alarm among the world com-munity, prompting efforts to preserve what is left of this precious resource and the plants and animals that inhabit it.

In some respects our oceans have fared no better. Most of the sea-based oil pollution comes not from headline grabbing oil spills, but from routine practices in the shipping industry and recreational boating. Plastic trash, six-pack rings and bottles are thrown into the oceans by commercial fishermen and the public. This litter pollutes the water and chokes or traps marine life, killing sea turtles, young seals, birds and other species. Many species of marine life have been harvested so extensively that they are in danger of extinction.

In addition, many countries continue to dump raw sewage and garbage in the ocean.

Preservation of the earth's wildlife and natural resources isn't a concern only for companies using resources from the rain forest, harvesting our oceans, or mining our earth. All businesses can do their part to preserve the environment, even in their local communities. Reducing the use of paper saves trees. Wisely adjusting thermostats uses less energy, saving natural gas, oil or coal. Proper disposal of hazardous wastes protects ground and surface waters. Supporting programs that set aside land for wildlife habitats and limited recreation helps assure natural environments will continue to exist so people will be able to stay in touch with nature. Other companies' efforts are detailed in the following case studies.

ITT Sheraton : Responsibility Begins "At Home"

At its Boston headquarters, the ITT Sheraton Corporation has designed policies to minimize the impact of its operations on the environment throughout its global network of nearly 450 hotels, inns, resorts and all-suites operating in 62 countries. ITT Sheraton, as a high profile representative of the industrialized world doing business in developed and developing nations, sees itself as being in a position to set an example for others.

For ITT Sheraton, environmental responsibility truly "begins at home." A paper recycling program at the corporation's headquarters had the following results for 1990, and the program continues to become more effective each year: 120 tons of paper separated, 2,040 trees saved, 300 barrels of oil saved (25 barrels saved for each ton of paper made from recycled material versus paper manufactured from wood pulp), and more than 237,000 cubic yards of paper diverted from landfill sites.

In addition, ITT Sheraton is very proud of its wildlife and environmental fund-raising program called "Going Green," which was launched by its Africa and Indian Ocean division on World Animal Day in October 1989. This program is aimed at educating Sheraton guests about the environment and wildlife preservation while soliciting their financial support. It's a simple plan that has been tremendously successful.

Sheraton properties in that division promote the Optional Dollar Program as part of their "Going Green" campaign. The program invites all guests to add one dollar to their final bill when checking out. Sheraton then matches this amount in local currency and, with the help of the World Society for the Protection of Animals (WSPA) and the Marine Conservation Society, selects local projects as recipients of the total funds. As of early 1991, ITT Sheraton had raised $158,000 as a result of the Optional Dollar Program at its hotels in Uganda, Zimbabwe, Nigeria, Zaire, Seychelles, Guinea Bissau, Djibouti, Benin and Botswana.

"We are delighted with this tremendous first year result," said Michael Prager, Sheraton's vice president and director of marketing, Africa and Indian Ocean region. "It reflects not only the generosity of our hotel guests, but also a growing awareness of the need for responsible tourism, which we hope to increasingly cultivate among travellers."

With proceeds from the program, Sheraton recently donated two Land Rovers and anti-poaching equipment to a project at the Yankari National Park in Nigeria. This has resulted in a decrease in poaching and a recovery of animal numbers. To encourage the breeding of young tortoises in the Seychelles, Sheraton has raised funds to build a tortoise nursery. A minor but effective effort also has been made by the Sheraton Gaborone Hotel and Towers. They are collecting and recycling tin cans and using the monies received for tree planting.

What's in it for ITT Sheraton?

By helping to preserve and protect the earth's wildlife and natural resources, ITT Sheraton is helping to save the subjects of natural beauty and wonders that many people travel to see. In addition, they are taking active steps to become a model citizen and exemplary corporate neighbor at all of their worldwide locations.

Arizona Public Service Provides Safe
Landings For Harris Hawks

Arizona Public Service Company (APS), based in Phoenix, Arizona, became concerned about Harris Hawks and other large birds of prey coming into contact with its overhead power lines in the eastern part of the metropolitan Phoenix area. To prevent potential electrocutions, the utility formed a Raptor Protection Program.

The larger the bird's wingspan, the greater the potential it has for getting into trouble as it alights on power lines. As they land, the birds make contact with energized equipment, creating an electrical contact that can injure or kill them.

In 1990, the company began installing rubber hose-like birdguards over the wires entering the transformers and other equipment attached to its electrical distribution system. It also built special perches on the top of some of the power poles in areas where the birds frequently land, especially in the Arizona desert where the poles are the highest points.

The birdguards and perches significantly reduced the number of bird contacts, and APS estimates that the Raptor Protection Program eliminates 98 percent of potential electrocutions. In addition, the program reduces the number of power outages and maintenance problems that can result from such contacts. APS is expanding the Raptor Protection Program to include protective devices on additional selected facilities in its statewide system.

The National Environmental Awards Council recently honored and recognized APS for its Raptor Protection Program. The Council's members include the Nature Conservancy, the National Audubon Society, the Humane Society of the United States, the National Wildlife Federation and others.

In several communities that APS serves, the company also helps local residents with their soil conservation efforts. The utility regularly trims trees to keep them clear of power lines.

The trimmings then are sent through a wood chipper and ground into mulch. Rather than hauling the mulch generated by their regular tree trimming work to a local landfill, APS provides the mulch at no charge to the public. The mulch is used to prevent soil erosion, control weeds and minimize dust.

APS now gets more requests for the chips and mulch than it can fill, and saves the $35 it was spending for each load it was taking to the landfill.

What's in it for APS?

National recognition for its Raptor Protection Program, which preserves wildlife, prevents power outages and minimizes maintenance problems on overhead power lines. Its tree trimming program saves the company hauling and landfill fees, and builds goodwill within the community.

Tree Saver, Inc. Puts Preservation In The Bag

A mother's concern about securing an environmentally safe future for her children prompted Trisha Hood of Denver, Colorado to found Tree Saver Inc. in 1989. After wrestling with the choice of "paper or plastic" bags at the grocery stores, Hood got the idea for her first product, a reusable unibody canvas grocery bag, at a seminar on the environment.

The design for the prototype was launched on the laundry room floor of their home with assistance from her two children. It incorporated the sturdy handles from the plastic bag and square bottom from the paper bag. She took samples of the new canvas bags to local health food stores and was pleasantly surprised with the response from store owners.

What started as a personal commitment to do what she could to protect the environment quickly turned into a successful business. Local seamstresses were contracted to produce enough bags to keep up with the demand, which grew steadily as grocery stores also became interested in offering customized bags for sale to their customers.

"It was so timely," Hood said. "The bag really sold itself. It's great because it is a durable product that satisfies a common need, and it enables every consumer to be a part of the solution to help protect and preserve our environment."

Canvas grocery bags can go a long way in preserving our natural resources, according to Hood. The 100 percent cotton bags are sewn with 100 percent cotton thread. They are reusable, biodegradable, washable and have a life span of five to seven years. Unlike plastic and paper bags, canvas bags do not lead to deforestation, depletion of nonrenewable resources, acid rain nor soil, air and water contamination.

Hood's concern for the environment goes beyond the Tree Saver products. "I am very interested in educating everyone, especially children, about solutions to environmental problems," she said. "We are very involved with the schools and it is part of our company philosophy to commit volunteer time towards education and sharing environmental information. My reward for that effort is the letters I get, especially from the children."

Tree Saver's product line is now sold nationwide and has been expanded to include reusable canvas lunch bags, oxford nylon cloth, reusable trash can liners and nylon tetoncloth blend reusable dry cleaning bags. Although they are not biodegradable, the nylon bags are designed to last for years.

"A lot of what Tree Saver has done to be successful is to get the idea out to consumers and businesses," Hood said. "Selling canvas bags and encouraging their use has become an important part of the image many companies want to portray to their customers. Canvas bags are a visible way to show that you are concerned about the environment."

What's in it for Tree Saver, Inc.?

Providing products that conserve resources and eliminate waste brings a great deal of satisfaction to everyone involved at Tree Saver, Inc., as well as generates projected sales of $150,000 for 1992.

Starkist Pledges Dolphin Safe Tuna

For a number of years, StarKist Seafood Company had been concerned about the accidental killing and injury of dolphins during tuna fishing operations. In April 1990, it announced a sweeping new policy to save dolphin lives and protect them from injury. With this policy, StarKist became the first major American tuna company to make a commitment to the public to sell only "Dolphin Safe" tuna.

As a result of this policy, StarKist will not buy any tuna that is caught at the expense of killing dolphins. Labels on StarKist tuna cans now carry the "Dolphin Safe" symbol and message, "No harm to dolphins," to inform consumers of StarKist's commitment to the safety of this marine species.

The "Dolphin Safe" policy also ensures that StarKist will continue to refuse to buy any fish caught with gill or drift nets. Drift nets are virtually undetectable nylon nets, as large as 40 miles in length. They are hazardous to many forms of aquatic life because they are not selective. Birds, dolphins, sea turtles and other marine animals, including certain types of whales, can be snared along with the intended catch.

StarKist will only buy tuna caught by "Dolphin Safe" fishing practices. The major tuna fishing method used throughout the world is purse seining because it has enabled fishermen to increase their tuna catch by a factor of 10. A purse seine net has a cable threaded at the bottom of it, much like the drawstring on a purse. The top of the net has cork floats which keep the net secured at the ocean's surface. Once the tuna are located, the ship circles the school and drops the net in its wake. After the net is around the entire school, the cable is tightened and the net closes underneath the catch.

Purse seining can be "Dolphin Safe" as long as the net is not set on the dolphins -- a sometimes difficult task in the bountiful Eastern Tropical Pacific Ocean. This coastal zone extending from Southern California to Chile is the only region in the world where dolphins are known to naturally swim above schools of yellow fin tuna. This natural phenomenon makes an easy way for fishermen to locate tuna, but there are other ways fisherman can locate tuna to avoid coming in contact with dolphins. They can use other signs to locate tuna such as stirrings at the surface of the water, sea birds or by using electronic gear.

StarKist, as a leading brand of tuna, has taken a leadership role with its "Dolphin Safe" policy, thereby encouraging the fishing industry to make tuna fishing safer for dolphins around the world.

What's in it for StarKist?

StarKist has earned customer confidence and support by being responsive to the public's concern about dolphins. Environmental groups, including the Earth Island Institute and Greenpeace, are among those that have praised StarKist's action.

Monsanto Plants A Forest In Wales

The Monsanto Company, headquartered in St. Louis, Missouri, will have created a forest in Wales by the winter of 1992. As part of a regulation to maintain a buffer zone between its Newport chemical plant and nearby neighborhoods, Monsanto is developing and planting nearly 70 acres of woodlands and wetlands. Although it takes Nature thousands of years to bring a new forest into the world, the Monsanto project will create the new habitat in just a few years.

Monsanto, following recommendations from the Forestry Commission, is planting the forest with nearly 40,000 trees and shrubs from about 15 different varieties. Their forest will include British hardwoods such as oak, cherry and ash, and smaller trees like the maple which will not present a problem to utility lines. The Newport plant also is working with the Royal Society for the Protection of Birds to develop two lakes which will encourage amphibious birds to settle in the new habitat. It is hoped that the new forest will double its wildlife population within the first two or three years.

The forest has many environmental benefits. It will promote wild flora and fauna, as well as serve to reduce noise from the manufacturing area of the plant. It also will beautify the neighborhood and reduce carbon dioxide in the air.

In addition to the environmental benefits of the project, local schools have participated in portions of the plantings and future classes will be able to study the growth of many species and the forest itself over the years.

What's in it for Monsanto?

This forestation project is an example of how Monsanto fulfills its pledge to manage its corporate real estate, including plant sites, to benefit nature.

Vans Pines, Inc. Helps Companies Promote Tree Planting

Vans Pines, Inc., located in West Olive, Michigan, has been in business as a forest tree seedling nursery since the early 1930's. It's a business that realized the benefits of being "green" long before the environmental movement got its shot in arm with the 1970 Earth Day celebration.

As Gary Van Slooten, a third-generation Vans man explains about this family-owned business, "Grandmother is 91, and her philosophy has always been 'Now is a good time to plant,' and that's true now more than ever. Trees are great for our environment."

Vans Pines plants and nurtures 125 different species of evergreens and deciduous trees. At any one time, they have between 27-30 million seedlings in their inventory. About half their stock is native to the area, but they also import seeds from around the world. Their traditional customers had been foresters, landscapers, other nurseries and growers, until something different began to happen.

"Promoting tree planting became a very positive thing. Companies began using seedlings as promotions to build goodwill with their customers, the public, and to help the environment," he said. "Our first customer was J.L. Hudson, now the Dayton Corporation. They gave away 100,000 trees in 1970."

Other companies have joined in. Van Slooten recalls a 1971 promotion by General Electric that gave away 1 million trees, and a lumber store in the Chicago area that has handed out 10,000 trees each year since 1970 for Earth Day celebrations. During 1991, General Mills gave away at least 360,000 trees through a promotion with its Lucky Charms product.

"It sold cereal for General Mills, gave them a better environmental stance with the population, and we got 360,000 people to plant trees," Van Slooten said. "We're helping to re-green America. Even though our business motives are economical, the benefits are still there. After all, it's a healthy way for business to plant a lasting impression."

What's in it for Vans Pines?

In addition to its steady nursery business, Vans Pines generates considerable income by supplying seedlings for another market -- companies that want to help the environment and their public relations image by offering tree seedlings to plant as part of their business promotion.

Herman Miller: Takes Stand To Preserve The Rain Forests

Herman Miller, Inc., based in Zeeland, Michigan, is an international firm engaged primarily in the manufacture and sale of office systems, products and related services. Its reputation as a furniture maker is surpassed only by the long standing recognition it has received for its many environmental initiatives.

In March 1990, the company announced that tropical woods, which cannot be obtained from sustained-yield forest sources, were being eliminated from Herman Miller's standard products. That meant its signature piece, the Eames lounge chair, would only be offered in alternative veneers, such as walnut and cherry, when the company's existing supply of rosewood was depleted. Since its introduction in the 1950's, the Eames lounge chair, designed by Charles and Ray Eames and manufactured by Herman Miller, has been made with rosewood obtained from South American sources.

"We share in the growing worldwide concern about tropical rain forests," said Richard H. Ruch, chief executive officer. "Rain forests are a critical resource for people around the world, benefiting us ecologically and providing valuable raw materials and by-products to many industries."

How the change in materials will affect sales of Eames chairs is unknown, but Herman Miller believes it was the right thing to do. Such a decision is not surprising for a company like Herman Miller, where environmentally sound policies have saved money for the company while helping to save the earth.

In 1982, Herman Miller built an $11 million waste-to-energy heating and cooling plant which saves them $750,000 a year in fuel and landfill costs. The company's efforts to reduce have resulted in annual savings of $1.4 million. Its recycling program, which even includes buying back used office furniture that can be reconditioned and resold, has saved $900,000 a year.

Its efforts do not go unnoticed. In November 1991, President George Bush recognized Herman Miller as one of five citation winners for environmental quality management. The citation was given as part of the first President's Environment and Conservation Challenge Awards. Earlier in 1991, Herman Miller was honored for its long-standing and exemplary environmental initiatives at the fifth annual America's Corporate Conscience Awards given by the Council on Economic Priorities.

What's in it for Herman Miller?

Bottom line annual savings of at least $3 million per year and national recognition as a true friend of the environment.

HOW YOUR BUSINESS CAN DO IT, TOO!

PRESERVATION OF NATURAL RESOURCES AND WILDLIFE is a responsibility of all of us if future generations are to enjoy life as we know it. The balance between the needs of mankind and the needs of the earth's creatures and our environment is a delicate one that requires our constant attention. Neither businesses nor consumers can continue to take from the earth without regard for its wildlife, plant life and mineral formations.

Even if your business does not make direct use of natural resources such as lakes, oceans or streams, coal or other fossil fuels, trees or forests, or wildlife, there are ways to help preserve our environment.

Place a ✔ in the box next to the activities you can implement in your daily business operations. Then, list them in the back of the book.

☐ Plant Trees

Trees help clean the air and can provide much needed shade on a hot summer day. Check the landscaping of your property to see if trees can enhance the area. If you are leasing space, perhaps other tenants can join you in your request to the property management for more low-water use greenery suitable for your climate.

☐ It's In The Bag

Provide your customers an alternative to plastic or paper bags by offering canvas shopping bags for sale. The bags are available from several different suppliers and can be imprinted with your company name or logo. They can also be used as a premium or sales incentive for special promotions.

☐ From Seedlings Big Trees Will Grow

Many companies have realized significant marketing benefits through promotions in which they give tree seedlings to their customers. Customers get a free tree, and the company gains recognition for its effort to help the environment. But most of all, more trees get planted!

☐ Cut The Rings

Before disposing of plastic six-pack rings or other similar packaging, snip each circle so the packaging cannot become a danger to wildlife.

☐ Report Illegal Dumping

Ignoring the illegal practices of other companies only makes it worse for businesses who are complying with regulations. Even though bad publicity usually is generated about the practices of some businesses when offenders are caught and fined, the public will support those companies that use proper disposal methods. Because the environment suffers from illegal dumping, responsible business owners should take action to stop it.

☐ Support Companies That Are Environmentally Sensitive

The Council on Economic Priorities and other groups routinely evaluate companies and recognize those with favorable and unfavorable environmental records. Establish business relationships with companies that take a stand to preserve and protect the earth.

☐ Save Trees, Buy Recycled Paper Products

Purchase recycled paper. Stock the cafeteria with napkins and paper towels made from recycled paper; buy restroom supplies made from recycled paper; and select recycled paper products for all other office needs, from copy paper and stationery to promotional literature.

☐ Composting

Composting can be a viable alternative for many companies dealing with agricultural or food products, or landscaping debris. If you're not sure how to begin, or how to evaluate the benefits of composting, contact a local expert at a university or government office for assistance. If you're not interested in doing it yourself, find a local company that will haul away your composting material free of charge in return for the raw materials used for their compost product.

☐ Support Projects That Protect Wildlife or Replenish Natural Resources

Even if your business operations or products don't directly affect wildlife or use natural resources, you still can show your commitment. Get involved with a campaign or sponsorship. Donate trees for planting in a public park. Conduct a promotion whereby a percentage of the proceeds from sales of your product or service will be donated to a conservation organization or to a regional campaign to preserve a certain animal species. Get employees involved in a program to clean a local stream, stretch of beach, forest recreation area or mountain preserve. Contact the local news media to alert them to your efforts.

Chapter 8

Special Environmental Measures & Activities

"We have long been active in supporting conservation and in safeguarding our environment, especially the oceans and seas around the world, where we harvest seafood every day."

Jeffery J. O'Hara
President
Red Lobster

"Target believes that caring about the environment is an important commitment that we all must make."

Ann Aronson
Manager,
Environmental Programs
Target Stores

"Americans see the water quality problem as warranting drastic action. And, according to our survey, many of them are getting involved at a grass roots level, where they can really make a difference."

Peter H. Coors
President
Coors Brewing Company

The environmental movement, although two decades old, is exerting more influence now than ever before. As a result, business and industry are responding positively in many different ways, from changing their packaging to giving away pine seedlings, from setting up educational programs to opening public recycling facilities.

Despite all the information and all we have learned about environmental matters since the early 1970's, saving the earth remains a complex challenge with no one, easy solution. There are, however, many simple steps that individuals and businesses can take. The previous chapters presented information on what some companies have done in a specific area like recycling, conservation, waste management, pollution and toxin elimination, preserving our wildlife or developing environmentally safe products.

Other companies have taken special actions to make a contribution to saving the earth. Some of these programs are included in this chapter.

Natural Product Corp. Uses Waste Exchange To Find Raw Materials

Natural Product Corp., a Shippensburg, Pennsylvania company, found an economical source for raw materials by using the Northeast Industrial Waste Exchange, one of a dozen or more waste exchanges throughout the country that helps companies buy and sell trash.

"The exchange proved to be a great resource for us," said Michael Lanasa, president of Natural Product Corp. "We noticed Quaker Maid, a furniture division of White Consolidated Industries located in Leesport, Pennsylvania, had listed scrap wood, which we wanted to use as fuel."

The connection was made and the contract was signed. Every six weeks, Quaker Maid delivered 15,000 pounds of scrap wood to Natural Product. Natural Product soon found a better use for the scrap wood than burning it. The wood became the raw material used for birdhouse kits. Thanks to this exchange, Natural Product developed a new product, and Quaker Maid realized savings of about $2,000 per year.

Other raw materials the company uses to produce useful products include textile waste and waste liner paper. The textile waste is used for making scented coasters called "Mug Mates," and the waste liner paper is converted to 3" X 3" envelopes, scented auto tags and drawer liners.

The Environmental Protection Agency lists at least a dozen US regional exchanges that publish listings of companies interested in buying, selling or exchanging waste.

What's in it for Natural Product Corp.?

The opportunities to turn the waste of another business into new, profitable consumer products, as well as a good feeling for engaging in socially conscious business activities which directly help the bottom line.

Fuji Grant Protects South Carolina Wetlands

Fuji Photo Film USA has teamed up with a photographer and The Nature Conservancy to help protect an unspoiled habitat in the South Carolina wetlands. The valuable ACE Basin where the Ashepoo, Combahee and Edisto rivers come together, about 45 miles south of Charleston, South Carolina, is one of the most pristine and diverse such areas on the Atlantic Coast.

This basin provides a safe winter home for ducks migrating on the Atlantic Flyway, and is home to other animals such as bald eagles, loggerhead sea turtles, American alligators and short-nosed sturgeons, an endangered species of fish.

Fuji is a co-sponsor, with The Nature Conservancy, of the ACE Basin Book Project, a documentation of the basin by Charleston photographer Thomas Blagden, Jr. The book will educate readers about the basin and help raise funds to protect it from future development.

"This project is important for Fuji on many levels," said Osamu "Sam" Inoue, president, Fuji Photo Film USA, Inc. "Fuji has always been concerned with nature and the global environment, and the ACE Basin Book Project is a wonderful opportunity to make a difference. It's also very gratifying to support a project that uses photography to sway public opinion for such a worthwhile cause. And finally, South Carolina is the home of Fuji's first US factory."

What's in it for Fuji?

An opportunity to help protect the environment by using its products to educate and enlighten.

First Brands Glad Bags And City Of Chicago: Curbside Recycling Is "In The Bag"

Faced with Environmental Protection Agency guidelines, as well as state mandates, cities from Chicago to Pittsburgh to Mobile have been struggling to successfully implement recycling programs. Now, one year after implementing the Blue Bag program designed by First Brands Corporation, scores of cities -- including Chicago, Pittsburgh and Mobile -- see that problem as solved.

First Brands, maker of GLAD Wrap and Bags, designed special blue recycling bags for the Blue Bag Program. "After more than 25 years of working with municipal managers to develop solutions to solid waste issues, we have an understanding of municipal needs," said Patrick O'Brien, First Brands corporate director of Environmental Affairs.

"Bags allow municipalities an easier way to have recycling as part of their long-term solid waste planning. A bag-based program seems to solve many of the problems associated with traditional rigid container recycling programs," O'Brien said.

"We've been told by city managers, recycling coordinators and haulers that the program saves money, time and retraining costs, and encourages higher diversion rates."

At curbside, the bag-based program reduces windborne litter, insect problems and weather-related difficulties associated with open-topped containers. Since the recycling bag is bright "see-thru" blue, sanitation workers can easily determine that it contains recyclable materials.

At pickup, the bag-based program allows municipalities to use existing equipment and crews, and eliminates personnel retraining as well as curbside sorting currently associated with most bin-based systems. Since bags are one-way pickups, field tests show that the program offers significant time/motion savings. Cities using the bag-based program have discovered that the recycling bags hold up under compaction.

When the bag-based program is compared to an open-bin program, the savings are dramatic. According to David Robinson, Chicago's recycling coordinator, "The overriding reason we went with the bag-based program is an economic one; the high cost of other recycling programs didn't make sense. We conducted a 62,000 household test using bins, and found that collecting recyclables using this method costs twice what landfilling the waste would."

He says that the Blue Bag Program will cost the city $13 million. But he says, if the city used bins and offered separate collection, the cost would be $40 million -- three times the cost of the bag-based system. "We'll be able to use our existing fleet and crews, and the Blue-Bag Program will fit into our existing operations," he says. "We don't have new vehicle expenses, added labor costs, or the charges for bins and bin delivery."

What's in it for the City of Chicago?

Chicago estimates it will save $27 million with the blue bag system and have an easy and convenient method for residents to participate in a citywide recycling program.

Coors Brewing Company Helps Clear America's Water

The Coors Brewing Company, located in Golden, Colorado, has a keen interest in water quality. While the Clean Water Act of 1972 and Safe Drinking Water Act of 1974 prompted significant improvements in our nation's water supply, Coors was concerned that if increased efforts were not undertaken during the decade of the 90's, many of the gains obtained over the past 20 years might be reversed.

In 1990, Coors acted on its concerns. In association with the Center for Resource Management, Coors launched Pure Water 2000, a national water conservation, preservation and cleanup program geared toward increased public awareness and grass roots action. Components of Coors Pure Water 2000 are threefold: support of local water projects nationwide, a public awareness campaign and an outreach program to a wide range of environmental organizations.

Working closely with its extensive distributor network, Coors Pure Water 2000 provides grants to local water cleanup and preservation projects nationwide.

"We don't pretend to be environmental experts at Coors. Rather, we provide local environmental groups -- the real experts -- with the resources they need to make a difference in their community's water quality," said Peter H. Coors, president of Coors Brewing Company. "In the program's first year, we provided financial support and other resources for more than 300 such projects."

In 1990, Coors Pure Water 2000 projects ranged from local cleanups along lakes, rivers and beaches to long-range wetlands and wildlife habitat restoration programs and regional water conservation projects.

"Riverkeeper" and "Soundkeeper" programs for the Hudson River and Long Island Sound in New York, as well as the Puget Soundkeeper program in Seattle, Washington, are unique projects of Coors Water 2000. In each case, Coors and its local distributors have donated funds to purchase boats and hire personnel to patrol the respective waterways and monitor water quality.

Examples of other key projects include the nationwide Freshwater Initiative in which Coors, as a corporate partner with The Conservation Fund and the National Geographic Society, provides a five-year, $50,000 commitment to undertake research and education programs to increase understanding of freshwater issues. In Arizona, Arkansas and Texas, Coors and its distributors have teamed up to support various Adopt-A-Shore/Beach/Lake or Highway programs.

Coors' interest in the environment goes beyond the Pure Water 2000 program. Since 1970, Coors has collected 1.75 billion pounds of aluminum cans and has paid out $395 million to customers for their recycled cans. Its ride sharing program, established in the 1970's, was awarded the President's 1980 Energy Efficiency Award. Today, more than 600 employees participate in the program, including more than 115 who vanpool in the 13 vehicles purchased by Coors.

What's in it for the Coors Brewing Company?

Pure Water 2000 enables Coors to become partners with local environmental groups across the country to preserve and protect water, one of our most important natural resources and a necessary ingredient in Coors' products. The program generates results, as well as enhances Coors' reputation as a corporation that is concerned about the environment.

Browning-Ferris Industries Teaches Tourists About Trash

In the San Francisco Bay area, there's one tourist attraction that's garbage -- but it's one you won't want to miss. It's The Recyclery, an $11 million integrated waste handling operation that also promotes public recycling and education.

The Recyclery, built by Browning-Ferris Industries, Inc., based in Houston, Texas, is a showcase of environmental ingenuity. Its $1 million Education Center includes one-of-a-kind interactive electronic displays and a striking 100-foot-long "Wall of Garbage" that represents just three minutes worth of trash generated by the surrounding community.

Other exhibits include Garbage History, a look at how our ancestors solved their waste disposal problems; Shoot the Loot, where visitors can zap recyclable materials with a light gun; Buried Treasure, which takes a look at how much could be recovered from landfills; and Magnet Fishing, which demonstrates the magnetic properties of different metals.

The heart of The Recyclery is a $10 million Materials Recovery Facility with state-of-the-art equipment for commercial recycling. The 80,000 square-foot facility can process up to 1600 tons of refuse from local businesses daily, recovering more than 70 percent of that for recycling. The Recyclery also has a public Buy-Back Center that accepts 38 types of materials including aluminum, paper, plastics and cardboard.

What's in it for Browning-Ferris?

The Materials Recovery Facility of The Recyclery demonstrates the commitment Browning-Ferris Industries is making to implement environmentally responsible methods of operating its waste management business. The $1 million Education Center is viewed as an investment in our future by helping people understand the advantages of recycling and its benefits to the environment.

Target Stores Target Kids To Save Our Earth

Target is actively reducing, reusing and recycling wherever possible at its stores across the country. But its environmental program truly has an eye to the future. Target is the founding international sponsor of "Kids for Saving Earth," a program started by Clinton Hill, a young boy from Minnesota, for a group of his sixth grade friends.

Clinton lived a short life, dying at age 11 of cancer, but his optimism, enthusiasm and belief that kids could be part of the pollution solution lives on with help from Target. As sponsor of "Kids for Saving Earth," a nonprofit organization, Target provides extensive information for kids and teachers on how to start their own clubs. They publish and distribute quarterly "Kids for Saving Earth" newspapers to various clubs and through their stores. The colorful newspapers, printed on recycled paper, are full of environmental tips and activities to keep the clubs busy.

Target also provides a space in its stores where kids can display their "Kids for Saving Earth" activities, or conference rooms where clubs can meet. During the week of Earth Day 1990, half a million people signed the "Kids for Saving Earth" promise at Target stores across the country. The signatures were then presented to the United Nations Youth Forum for the Environment in New York City.

"Kids for Saving Earth" clubs teach kids that they can make a difference, even by taking minor steps, such as conserving water at home, recycling, carpooling or riding their bikes. The first club was founded in 1989, and 18 months later there were 12,000 clubs with 300,000 members in 16 different countries worldwide! Kids truly are interested in learning how they can save the earth.

What's in it for Target?

Target is a family-oriented store that is committed to helping children learn about our environment and act upon their desire to preserve the world. As part of the Dayton Hudson Corporation, Target participates in the corporation's practice of giving 5 percent of its pretax profits to nonprofit organizations in its communities. Many of the "Kids For Saving Earth" activities also generate foot traffic in Target stores.

Arizona Partnership Opens Recycling Hotline

Quick information on what, where and how to recycle is at the fingertips of Arizona residents, thanks to a public-private partnership.

The Arizona Recycling Hotline, (602) 253-2687 or (602) CLEANUP or (800) 94-REUSE, is an automated, environmental clearinghouse that centralizes and dispenses information from different government agencies, private enterprises, nonprofit groups and other resources. The service is provided to callers, free of charge and without taxpayer funding.

The Arizona Recycling Hotline was developed by Chris Warner, a Phoenix business consultant, to operate through a UNIX computer system. Eight Arizona businesses, including local radio station KNIX, NBC affiliate station KPNX-TV and Arizona Public Service Company, were the initial sponsors when the Hotline made its debut in late 1991.

Callers to the Hotline simply enter their zip code into the system to get recorded information on the nearest recycling location for materials from aluminum to motor oil. After entering a zip code, the caller gets an environmental tip and is asked to enter the desired access code, which may be the sponsor's name or call letters.

The caller is then welcomed by the sponsor to the "Official State of Arizona Recycling Hotline" and is asked to select from four options: general information, community programs, drop off or buy back facilities and bulletin board/sponsor messages. Callers also may leave messages for the sponsor.

What's in it for Arizona?

Residents receive access to current information on recycling and recycling facilities in Arizona.

Honeywell Helps Schools Get Smart About Energy

Honeywell Inc., headquartered in Minneapolis, Minnesota, helps more than 750 American school districts save money on energy bills while creating a comfortable and cost-efficient environment for their students and teachers. Their School Services Program has saved millions of dollars for participating schools by helping them operate more efficiently. The savings schools achieve through the program can be applied to teaching and learning, rather than utility bills.

Schools enter into a partnership with Honeywell, in which Honeywell conducts an energy audit and develops a list of possible ways to reduce energy costs. The list might include repairing and updating HVAC and lighting systems, maintenance and operation of those systems, application of computerized energy management, integration of fire and life safety systems, indoor air quality diagnostics, vendor services coordination and customized training for staff at the school. Honeywell guarantees in writing that the cost of upgrades will be paid for by the energy savings realized by improved operating efficiency and conserved energy. Since the program is self-funding, school districts have adequate cash flow to meet project payments. If their funds fall short at any time, Honeywell will make up the difference.

The Hemet Unified School District in California realized great results from the program. Limited funds prohibited the District from modernizing their facilities by traditional means. With the help of Honeywell, they were able to complete an extensive retrofit to improve classroom conditions in 14 school buildings. The school district will realize more than $5.4 million in energy savings, operational savings and utility rebates over the next 10 years, more than enough to meet project costs.

What's in it for Honeywell?

Honeywell helps aging schools improve their energy management and save money on energy costs as part of its commitment to the education of future generations.

HOW YOUR BUSINESS CAN DO IT, TOO!

SPECIAL ENVIRONMENTAL MEASURES AND ACTIVITIES can provide unlimited opportunities for your business to save the earth and gain positive public recognition. With a little creativity, planning and involvement of your employees, your special activities can be a great success in many ways.

Place a ✔ in the box next to the activities you can implement. Then, list them in the back of the book.

☐ Get Your Vendors Involved

Ask your vendors and suppliers to take up the cause and join your efforts. For example, initiate a partnership whereby your vendors agree to reduce their packaging. Advise them that you reserve the right to cancel contracts with them if they are found to be in violation of any applicable environmental regulations at the federal, state or local level.

☐ Tell It To The Leaders

Contact community leaders and ask for their commitment in implementing public recycling or other environmental programs. Let them know that businesses in the community are concerned about the environment and are willing to join with the public sector to make positive things happen, without costly and excessive regulations.

☐ Teach Them Young

Offer your technical expertise or financial resources to help develop a curriculum to teach local children about how they can help save the earth. Offer to visit the classroom to talk about what your business is doing to save the earth. Better yet, arrange on-site tours for school groups or the public to visit your business. Invite the media.

☐ Tell Your Story

Communicate what you are doing to save the earth to all your constituents -- employees, customers and the public. Deliver messages in statement stuffers about your environmental activities. Articles in company newsletters can explain to your employees what your business is doing to help the environment. Appear on local radio talk shows or television programs to let the public know of your environmental activities and commitment.

☐ Become Involved In Your Community

Serve on a local committee or support community projects directed to the environment. Get to know other business leaders, public figures and legislators. Become knowledgeable on pressing local concerns. Is landfill space getting scarce? Can the community park use some new trees? What about a regional ride sharing plan or trip reduction campaign?

☐ Adopt-A-Cause

You'll need help from your employees with this one. But the effort can be great for team-building, camaraderie and company pride. For example, adopt a stretch of highway that a group of employees -- including management -- will routinely clean of litter. Adopt a forest and save an endangered animal species living there, or revitalize it by planting trees.

☐ Sponsor An Environmental Event

Many communities have Earth Day celebrations or other special events to bring attention to the environment. Perhaps your company can be a sponsor, or simply participate with a booth at which you can distribute information on your company's environmentally safe products or production methods.

Chapter 9

Government Support For Businesses That Save The Earth

Saving the earth is everyone's responsibility, and despite what some people may think, every effort made on behalf of the earth contributes to securing its future. In order for measurable progress to come about, however, businesses must be involved. Prodding business into actions that require financial investment, research and manpower can be accomplished by consumer demand, dwindling supplies of raw materials or government intervention through incentives or punitive actions.

While it seems that news about fines, penalties and government restrictions make the headlines more often than businesses might like, there are many government programs that try to encourage innovation and compliance, rather than simply mandate regulation and dole out punishment.

The list that follows by no means is inclusive of all government resources and programs in every state. But, it can serve as a starting point for your business in its search for information on what programs and resources are available in your area or at the national level that could deal with your particular environmental concerns.

U.S. ENVIRONMENTAL PROTECTION AGENCY
401 M Street SW, Washington, D.C. 20460

Green Lights
Global Change Division, U.S. Environmental Protection Agency
401 M Street SW, Washington, D.C. 20460 (202) 382-4992

Pollution Prevention Information Clearinghouse
PPIC Technical Support,8400 Westpark Drive, McLean, VA 22102 (703) 821-4800

Office of Pollution Prevention
U.S. Environmental Protection Agency
401 M Street SW (PM-219), Washington, D.C. 20460 (202) 245-3557

Office of Research and Development
U.S. Environmental Protection Agency
401 M Street SW (PM-681), Washington, D.C. 20460 (202) 475-7161

Office of Solid Waste
U.S. Environmental Protection Agency
401 M Street SW (PM-565), Washington, D.C. 20460 (202) 382-4807

Office of Toxic Substances, Industrial Toxics Project
U.S. Environmental Protection Agency
401 M Street SW, Washington, D.C. 20460 (202) 382-3829

Pollution Prevention Research
Engineering Laboratory, U.S. Environmental Protection Agency
26 West Martin Luther King Drive, Cincinnati, Ohio 45268 (513) 569-7215

REGION I (ME, NH, VT, MA, CT, RI)
U.S. Environmental Protection Agency Region I
Pollution Prevention Program
John F. Kennedy Federal Building
Boston, Massachusetts 02203 (617) 565-1155

REGION II (NJ, NY, PR)
U.S. Environmental Protection Agency Region II
Policy and Program Integration, Branch Office of Program Management
26 Federal Plaza, New York, New York 10278 (212) 264-4296

REGION III (DC, DE, MD, PA, VA, WV)
Environmental Assessment Branch, Environmental Services Divison
U.S. Environmental Protection Agency Region III
841 Chestnut Building(3ES43),Philadelphia, Pennsylvania 19107 (215) 597-8327

REGION IV (AL, FL, GA, KY, MS, NC, SC, TN)
Pollution Prevention Unit
U.S. Environmental Protection Agency Region IV
345 Courtland Street NE, Atlanta, Georgia 30365 (404) 347-7109

REGION V (IL, IN, MI, MN, OH, WI)
Pollution Prevention Coordinator
U.S. Environmental Protection Agency Region V
230 South Dearborn Street (5MA-14), Chicago, Illinois 60604 (312) 886-4158

REGION VI (AR, LA, NM, OK, TX)
Pollution Prevention Coordinator, Office of Planning and Evaluation
U.S. Environmental Protection Agency Region VI
1445 Ross Avenue (6M-P), Dallas, Texas 75202 (214) 655-6444

REGION VII (IA,KS, MO, NE)
Waste Management Division
U.S. Environmental Protection Agency Region VII
726 Minnesota Avenue, Kansas City, Kansas 66101 (913) 551-7050

REGION VIII (CO, MT, ND, SD, UT, WY)
U.S. Environmental Protection Agency Region VIII
999 18th Street, Suite 500, Denver, Colorado 80202-2466 (303) 293-1603

REGION IX (AZ, CA, NV)
Pollution Prevention Program
U.S. Environmental Protection Agency Region IX
75 Hawthorne Street (H-1-B), San Francisco, California 94105 (415) 744-2190

REGION X (AK, ID, OR, WA)
Planning, Policy, and Evaluation Branch, Hazardous Waste Policy Division,
U.S. Environmental Protection Agency Region X
1200 Sixth Avenue (MD-102), Seattle, Washington 98101 (206) 553-5810

ALABAMA

Alabama Department of Environmental Management
1751 Congressman W.L. Dickinson Drive
Montgomery, Alabama 36130 (205) 271-7700

ALASKA

Department of Environmental Conservation
Division of Environmental Quality
410 Willoughby Ave. #105, Juneau, Alaska 99811-1795 (907) 465-5162

Pollution Prevention Coordinator
Alaska Department of Environmental Conservation
410 Willoughby Ave. #105, Juneau, Alaska 99811-1795 (907) 465-5275

*The Alaska Department of Environmental Conservation provides waste reduction
workshops and on-site audits in rural communities.*

ARIZONA

Arizona Department of Environmental Quality
2005 N. Central Avenue, Phoenix, Arizona 85001-0600 (800) 234-5677

Arizona Recycling Coordinator
2005 North Central Avenue, Suite 403-C, Phoenix, Arizona 85004 (602) 257-6980

*This office provides information and publications including a Recycling Directory for
Maricopa County.*

ARKANSAS

Department of Pollution Control and Ecology
Solid Waste Management Division
80001 National Drive, Little Rock, Arkansas 72209 (501) 570-2169

Arkansas Industrial Development Commission
#1 Capitol Mall, Little Rock, AR 72201 (501) 682-1121

This commission operates a waste minimization and recycling program designed to help industries reduce the amount of waste they produce and recycle or exchange the waste they cannot eliminate. A 30 percent tax credit is available to companies buying recycling equipment. Arkansas also has a gross receipts tax exemption for equipment that prevents or reduces air or water pollution.

CALIFORNIA

Department of Conservation, Recycling Division
1025 P Street, Sacramento, California 95814 (916) 323-3743

California Environmental Protection Agency
555 Capitol Mall, Suite 235, Sacramento, California 95814 (916) 322-2866

The California EPA offers many positive-based programs: grants/loans, environmental audits, multimedia approaches, research and development and clearinghouses or other outreach mechanisms.

California's Tax Law offers businesses many incentives to encourage conservation and protect the environment. Different types of businesses may receive different types of incentives, depending upon whether they fall under the Personal Income Tax Law (PITL) for individuals, sole proprietorships and partnerships, or the Bank and Corporation Tax Law (B&CTL) for corporations. The following tax incentives are available only to corporations taxed under the B&CTL. Ride sharing Deduction - Corporate employers may claim business expense deductions for subsidizing employees commutation by ridesharing or alternative forms of transportation. Pollution Control Facilities - Corporations are entitled to a deduction for amortizing pollution control facilities located in California.

These other tax incentive programs are available to companies taxed under either of the tax laws.

Employer Ridesharing Tax Credit - If a company has 200 or more employees, they are entitled to a credit of up to 20 percent of the costs for the purchase or lease of commuter vehicles that are used as part of an employer-sponsored ridesharing incentive program.

Low-Emission Fuel Vehicle Credit - This credit can be used when new low-emission vehicles are purchased.

Solar Energy Tax Credit - A tax credit of up to 10 percent of the cost of a solar energy system installed on the premises and used for commercial purposes.

Recycling Equipment Credit - A credit equal to 40 percent of the cost of qualified property purchased on or after January 1, 1989 and before January 1, 1994.

Cogeneration and Alternative Energy Equipment - Taxpayers may get deductions for amortizing equipment used to produce or convert energy from cogeneration, solar energy, etc.

COLORADO

Department of Health
Division of Hazardous Materials and Waste Management
4210 East 11th Avenue, Denver, Colordado 80220 (303) 331-4830

Office of Energy Conservation
1675 Broadway, Ste. 1300, Denver, Colorado 80202-4613 (303) 620-4292

Recycle Colorado Program
This program encourages recycling and conservation within state government.

Colorado has several laws which address income tax credits, recycling, and energy conservation as well as legislation that mandates state government to increase its purchase of recycled paper and paper products up to 50 percent of all paper purchases by the year 1994.

Colorado is running a pilot travel reduction program. It also offers tax credits for the purchase of qualified equipment used in connection with the manufacture of products composed of postconsumer waste and for investments in plastic recycling technology.

CONNECTICUT

Department of Environmental Protection
165 Capitol Avenue, Rm. 161, Hartford, Connecticut 06106 (203) 566-2110

Connecticut legislation created a $10 million revolving loan fund for small businesses to use for pollution prevention activities; established an Environmental Business Assistance Office to provide technical assistance; and created a Department of Environmental Protection ombudsman to assist small businesses with permits, environmental programs and requirements.

DELAWARE

Department of Natural Resources and Environmental Control
89 Kings Highway, P.O. Box 1401, Dover, Delaware 19903 (302) 739-4403

Delaware is developing its "Green Industries Initiative" that will focus on financial and technical incentives for reduction of waste generation and the use of recycled materials in manufacturing processes.

DISTRICT OF COLUMBIA

District of Columbia, Solid Waste Disposal
2750 South Capitol Street SE , Washington, D.C. 20032 (202) 767-8512

FLORIDA

Florida Department of Environmental Regulation
Twin Towers Office Building
2600 Blair Stone Road, Tallahassee, Florida 32399-2400 (904) 488-4805

Examples of incentives offered by Florida are listed.

Recycling equipment purchased by private businesses used to recycle Florida source recovered materials is exempt from the state sales tax.

The Waste Reduction Assistance Program (WRAP) assists large and small businesses in their efforts to eliminate wastes.

Amnesty Days are offered to give small businesses and individuals the opportunity to get rid of small quantities of hazardous waste at no charge.

In 1989, ten grants totalling $750,000 were given to the private sector to encourage the development of innovative recycling technology.

GEORGIA

Department of Natural Resources, Solid Waste Management Program
3420 Norman Berry Drive, Hapeville, Georgia 30354 (404) 656-2836

Environmental Protection Division, Georgia Department of Natural Resources
Floyd Tower East, Suite 1154 205 Butler Street SW
Atlanta, Georgia 30334 (404) 656-7802

HAWAII

Department of Health, Litter Control Office
205 Koula Street, Honolulu, Hawaii 96813 (808) 548-3400

Department of Business, Economic Development and Tourism
P.O. Box 2359, Honolulu, Hawaii 96804 (808) 586-2406

Hawaii offers several incentives, including low cost loans for the construction of waste water treatment facilities, exemptions from real property taxes for pollution control facilities, and exemptions from state and general excise tax for the purchase and installation of air pollution control equipment. Tax credits are available for businesses that acquire equipment that minimizes or eliminates the need for burning fossil fuels.

IDAHO

Idaho Department of Health and Welfare, Division of Environmental Quality
1410 North Hilton Statehouse Mail, Boise, Idaho 83720-9000 (208) 332-0502

Idaho has several programs to encourage companies to reduce environmental pollution. The water program has a voluntary ground/surface water protection initiative to help agricultural operations avoid excessive water pollution which results from farming activities. The RCRA program publishes a comprehensive publication containing information on recycling companies. Idaho's constitution was amended in 1974 to allow counties to issue environmental pollution control revenue bonds to aid in the financing of facility pollution control projects. Idaho offers two specific tax incentives for pollution control equipment. Property devoted to the prevention of water or air pollution is exempt from property taxation. Equipment purchased to meet air and water quality standards for state or federal agencies also is exempt from Idaho sales tax.

ILLINOIS

Illinois Environmental Protection Agency, Division of Land Pollution Control
P.O. Box 19276, Springfield, Illinois 62794-9276

INDIANA

Indiana Department of Environmental Management
105 South Meridian Street, Indianapolis, Indiana 46206-6015 (317) 232-8172

In 1990, Indiana enacted two laws which include extensive provisions to assist citizens, businesses and local governments through task forces, grants and loans. Indiana also recognizes businesses for their efforts in pollution prevention and recycling through the Governor's Award Program.

IOWA

Department of Natural Resources, Waste Management Authority Division
1900 East Grand, Des Moines, Iowa 50319 (515) 281-8176

KANSAS

Department of Health and Environment, Bureau of Air and Waste Management
Building 740, Forbes Field Topeka, Kansas 66620-0001 (913) 296-1590

KENTUCKY

Department of Natural Resources, Division of Waste Management
18 Reilly Road, Frankfort, Kentucky 40601 (502) 564-6716

Natural Resources and Environmental Protection Cabinet
Capitol Plaza, 5th Floor, Office of the Secretary
Frankfort, Kentucky 40601 (502) 564-3350

Kentucky provides several incentives, including a state sales tax exemption for the purchase of pollution control equipment used for the purpose of air, noise, waste or water pollution control. Recent initiatives have created additional tax exemptions. Machinery used to increase the consumption of recycled materials is exempt from sales or use tax. Machinery used for recycling purposes is exempt from local property taxes.

An income tax credit has been created for persons who purchase recycling or composting equipment to be used exclusively in Kentucky to process postconsumer wastes. Bonds have been earmarked for the funding of projects that will create or expand markets for materials recovered or diverted from the solid waste stream.

The "Kentucky Partners" program offers free hazardous waste management reviews, an information exchange, a hotline, onsite evaluators and a waste exchange program.

LOUISIANA

Department of Environmental Quality, Office of the Secretary
Policy Analysis and Planning
P.O. Box 82263, Baton Rouge, Louisiana 70884-2263 (504) 765-0720

During the 1991 session, Louisiana passed several measures that exclude certain pollution control equipment from the 3 percent state sales tax and provide tax credits for the purchase of qualified recycling equipment. Louisiana also has an industrial tax exemption program that ties an industry's environmental record to its tax exemption. The program includes incentives such as environmental compliance, emission reductions, recycling, waste reduction, diversification and new jobs for high unemployment areas.

MAINE

Department of Environmental Protection
State House, Station 17, Augusta, Maine 04333 (207) 289-7688

The Office of Pollution Prevention serves as a public contact and clearinghouse on pollution prevention and coordinates activities with other agencies and entities. There are several types of incentives also available in Maine. A tax credit for 30 percent of the cost of machinery and/or equipment to implement solid waste reduction, recycling, or reuse programs is available. Contact the Maine Waste Management Agency at (207) 289-5300 for more information.

Loan guarantees and low interest loans for removal of underground storage tanks and loan guarantees for replacement of small malfunctioning wastewater disposal systems are available. Contact the Finance Authority of Maine (207) 623-3263 for information on the loan programs.

Exemptions on sale/use and property taxes for pollution control facilities associated with air and water pollution control are available. Contact a Tax Certification Officer at the Department of Environmental Protection, (207) 289-2811.

MARYLAND

Maryland Department of the Environment
Hazardous & Solid Waste Management, Administration Office of the Secretary
2500 Broening Highway, Building 40
Baltimore, Maryland 21224 (301) 631-3084

The Department of the Environment provides environmental regulation and services such as capital and annual funding, planning and technical assistance to communities and businesses to foster sound environmental management. The Office of Community Assistance coordinates the Department of Environment's community outreach activities and serves as the liaison and problem-solver for business and industry. A state business permitting guide, "Environmental Regulation: A Business Guide to the Department of the Environment's Permitting Process," is available from the Department of Environment.

MASSACHUSETTS

Executive Office of Environmental Affairs
100 Cambridge Street, Boston, Massachusetts 02202 (617) 727-9800

MICHIGAN

Office of Waste Reduction Services
Michigan Department of Commerce and Natural Resources
309 North Washington Street, Suite 103, Lansing, Michigan 48909 (517) 335-1178

State of Michigan Department of Treasury
Treasury Building, Lansing, Michigan 48922 (517) 373-3200

Michigan offers several tax incentives. Tangible personal property purchased and installed as a component part of an air or water pollution control facility is exempt from sales and use tax. There is an underground storage tank assurance fund to provide assistance in meeting the financial responsibility requirements of the federal solid waste disposal act.

MINNESOTA

Department of Revenue
10 River Park Plaza, St. Paul, Minnesota 55146-2230 (612) 296-3425

Office of Strategic and Long Range Planning, Environmental Quality Board
300 Centennial Building, 658 Cedar Street
St. Paul, Minnesota 55155 (612) 296-3985

Minnesota Department of Trade and Economic Development
Environmental Resources Development
900 American Center Building, 150 East Kellogg Boulevard
St. Paul, Minnesota 55101 (612) 297-1291

Minnesota Office of Waste Management
1350 Energy Lane, St. Paul, Minnesota 55108 (612) 649-5750
Toll free in Minnesota 1-800-652-9747

Minnesota Technical Assistance Program (612) 627-4646
Toll free in Minnesota 1-800-247-0015

Minnesota Pollution Control Agency
520 Lafayette Road, St. Paul, Minnesota 55155 (612) 296-6300

Minnesota tax incentives for environmental protection include a sales tax exemption for equipment used to process solid or hazardous waste at a qualifying resource recover facility. Other incentives are a credit against the motor fuels excise tax for fuel-grade alcohol blended with gasoline to produce gasohol and an exemption from local property tax for certain pollution control equipment.

The Minnesota Technical Assistance Program was created in 1984 to assist industry with waste management, waste reduction and pollution prevention. This service is free to any Minnesota business. Types of assistance available through this program include telephone assistance, on-site visits, student interns, information resources, presentations and seminars.

The Office of Waste Management is a nonregulatory agency responsible for implementation of the Toxic Pollution Prevention Act. It provides educational information, including the annual Minnesota Recycling Directory and The Resource. a monthly newsletter, as well as management of local government assistance programs. In 1991, $14 million was distributed to counties in Minnesota to help them increase their recycling programs. In July 1991, $2 million in grants and low-interest loans were awarded for projects aimed at improving markets and manufacturing processes for recycled materials. Another $2 million in grants will be awarded by 1993.

MISSISSIPPI

Mississippi Department of Environmental Quality
P.O. Box 10385, Jackson, Mississippi 39289-0385 (601) 961-5171

The Multimedia Waste Minimization Act is designed to subsidize the costs of conducting waste minimization analyses and studies and the development, purchasing and implementing of waste minimization technologies and procedures. Pollution control equipment is considered manufacturing machinery and is taxed at a rate of 1 1/2 percent instead of 6 percent.

MISSOURI

Department of Natural Resources Waste Management Program
P.O. Box 176, Jefferson City, Missouri 65102 (314) 751-3176

Department of Revenue, Tax Administration Bureau
P.O. Box 840, Jefferson City, Missouri 65105-0840 (314) 751-2836

Missouri provides an exemption from sales and use taxes for machinery, equipment, appliances and devices purchased or leased and used solely for the purpose of preventing, abating or monitoring air and water pollution.

MONTANA

Department of Health and Environmental Sciences
Solid and Hazardous Waste Bureau
Cogswell Building, Room 3201, Helena, Montana 59620 (406) 444-2821

Department of Revenue
Room 455 Sam W. Mitchell Building, Helena, Montana 59620 (406) 444-2460

Montana has nearly a dozen different tax incentives for business in wind energy, reclaimable materials, installation of energy conservation materials, use of organic fertilizer, production of gasohol, air and water pollution control equipment, clean coal technology and others.

NEBRASKA

Department of Environmental Control, Solid Waste Division
P.O. Box 98922, Lincoln, Nebraska 68509 (402) 471-4210

Department of Revenue
301 Centennial Mall South, P.O. Box 94818
Lincoln, Nebraska 68509-4818 (402) 471-2971

Nebraska statutes provide for a refund of sales and use taxes paid on pollution control facilities.

NEVADA

Department of Taxation
Capitol Complex, Carson City, Nevada 89710-0003 (702) 687-4892

Department of Conservation and Natural Resources
Division of Environmental Protection
123 West Nye Lane, Carson City, Nevada 89710 (702) 687-4670

Nevada has several tax incentives, including one for tax exemptions to any real or personal property used to control air or water pollution. Nevada also has a statute known as the "Green Belt Law" that helps maintain and preserve natural land by giving farmers an incentive to keep land agricultural instead of developing it. To promote energy conservation, Nevada offers tax exemptions for heating and cooling systems (for water, air, or producing electricity) that rely on solar, wind, waste or solid waste conversion as a power source. Recycling efforts can benefit from Nevada "in transit" property taxation laws that offer exemptions for business inventory property.

NEW HAMPSHIRE

Department of Environmental Sciences, Waste Management Division
6 Hazen Drive, Concord, New Hampshire 03301 (603) 271-2900

NEW JERSEY

Division of Hazardous Waste Management
New Jersey Department of Environmental Protection
401 East State Street (CN028), Trenton, New Jersey 08625 (609) 292-8341

Department of the Treasury, Division of Taxation CN240
Tenton, New Jersey 08646-0240 (609) 292-5185

Corporations are entitled to claim tax credits equal to 50 percent of the cost of equipment which has been certified by the Department of Environmental Protection to qualify as "recycling equipment."

NEW MEXICO

Environment Department, Harold Runnels Building
1190 St. Francis Drive, P.O. Box 26110
Santa Fe, New Mexico 87502 (505) 827-2850

NEW YORK

Department of Environmental Conservation
50 Wolf Road, Albany, New York 12233-7253 (518) 485-8400

New York State Department of Economic Development
Office of Recycling, Market Development (ORMD)
One Commerce Plaza, Albany, New York 12245 (518) 486-6291

Over the past several years, New York State has approved or awarded $20 million in loans and loan guarantees to New York companies to expand manufacturing capacity for recycling. It also has granted nearly $1 million for feasibility studies to explore new recycling technologies. The ORMD has helped "Buy Recycled" vendor shows and has sponsored cooperative marketing pilot projects to help communities market recyclables more effectively. From a tax standpoint, New York also offers two tax benefits to promote the purchase of pollution control equipment.

NORTH CAROLINA

Pollution Prevention Pays Program
North Carolina Department of Environment, Health, and Natural Resources
P.O. Box 27687, Raleigh, North Carolina 27611-7687

Department of Economic and Community Development
430 North Salisbury Street, Raleigh, North Carolina 27611 (919) 733-4962

NORTH DAKOTA

State Department of Health and Consolidated Laboratories
State Capitol, Judicial Wing, 2nd Floor, 600 East Boulevard Avenue
Bismark, North Dakota 58505-0200 (701) 224-2372

OHIO

Department of Natural Resources, Division of Litter Prevention and Recycling
Fountain Square Court F-2 , Columbus, Ohio 43224 (614) 265-7061

OKLAHOMA

Department of Health Solid Waste Services
1000 NE 10th Street, Oklahoma City, Oklahoma 73152 (405) 271-7159

OREGON

Department of Environmental Quality
811 SW 6th Avenue, Portland, Oregon 97204 (503) 229-6408

Pollution Control Tax Credit, Management Services Division
811 SW 6th Avenue, Portland, Oregon 97204 (503) 229-6484

Oregon Department of Energy
625 Marion Street NE, Salem, Oregon 97310 (503) 378-4040
Toll free in Oregon 1-800-221-8035

Oregon has incentives for businesses, public agencies and homeowners to save energy. All are described in free booklets available by calling the Department of Energy. Oregon offers business tax credits to cut energy use, recycle waste or use renewable resources.

PENNSYLVANIA

Department of Environmental Resources
Waste Reduction and Recycling Section
P.O. Box 2063, Harrisburg, Pennsylvania 17105-2063 (717) 787-7382

Commonwealth of Pennsylvania, Department of Revenue
Department 281061, Harrisburg, Pennsylvania 17128-1061 (717) 787-2121

Pennsylvania tax incentives include a capital stock tax exemption for assets used to salvage, recycle or reclaim used materials in the manufacturing process. Any water and/or air pollution control devices, bought and used by a Pennsylvania business which benefits the general public, are exempt from the State's capital stock tax. Also, Pennsylvania businesses engaged in the processing of used lubricating oils are exempt from paying taxes on the equipment used for those processing activities.

RHODE ISLAND

Department of Environmental Management
Office of Environmental Coordination
83 Park Street, Providence, Rhode Island 02903 (401) 277-3434

Department of Administration, Division of Taxation
One Capitol Hill, Providence, Rhode Island 02908-5800 (401) 277-3050

Ocean State Cleanup and Recycling (OSCAR)
Department of Environmental Management
83 Park Street Providence, Rhode Island 02903-1037
(401) 277-3434 1-800-CLEAN RI

Several handbooks for businesses on the reduction and recycling of commercial solid waste are available from OSCAR. Rhode Island has had tax incentives in the form of credits, rapid write-offs, deductions and sales tax exemptions since the late 1970's. Some of the items eligible for tax credits include solar and wind energy systems, energy conservation items such as insulation, caulking or weatherstripping, clock thermostats, waste heat recovery systems and cogeneration systems.

SOUTH CAROLINA

Department of Health and Environmental Control
Bureau of Solid and Hazardous Waste Management
2600 Bull Street, Columbia, South Carolina 29201 (803) 734-5200

SOUTH DAKOTA

Division of Environmental Health, Water & Natural Resources Department
Foss Building, Pierre, South Dakota 57501 (605) 773-3151

TENNESSEE

Department of Health and Environment, Division of Solid Waste Management
701 Broadway - Customs House, 4th Floor
Nashville, Tennessee 37247-3530 (615) 741-3424

TEXAS

Department of Health, Division of Solid Waste Management
1100 West 49th Street, Austin, Texas 78756 (512) 458-7271

Comptroller of Public Accounts
LBJ State Office Building, Austin, Texas 78774 (512) 463-4000

Texas has two recently adopted policies that provide incentives for Texas businesses. The state sales tax on manufacturing machinery and equipment for pollution control and recycling equipment and machinery is being phased out. By 1995, all such equipment purchases also will be exempt from local sales taxes. Expenses for services and equipment purchased to reduce and/or recycle waste are currently deductible in the determination of franchise tax liabilities. The addition of new pollution control equipment may not increase franchise tax liabilities based on permanent assets.

UTAH

Bureau of Solid & Hazardous Waste, Division of Environmental Health
288 North 1460, Salt Lake City, Utah 84116-0690 (801) 244-7831

VERMONT

Agency of Natural Resources, Department of Environmental Conservation
The Annex, 103 South Main Street
Waterbury, Vermont 05671-0405 (802) 244-5674

Real and personal property installed and operated to abate pollution to state waters is exempt from state property taxes.

VIRGINIA

Commonwealth of Virginia, Council on the Environment
903 Ninth Street Office Building, Richmond, Virginia 23219 (804) 786-4500

Department of Taxation
Richmond, Virginia 23282 (804) 367-2062

Virginia Waste Minimization Program
11th Floor, Monroe Building, 101 North 14th Street
Richmond, Virginia 23219 (804) 371-8716

Commonwealth of Virginia
Department of Economic Development
P.O. Box 798, Richmond, Virginia 23206-0798 (804) 371-8100

Certain certified pollution control equipment and facilities are exempt from retail sales and use tax. Certified pollution control, solar energy, generating and cogenerating equipment and facilities may be wholly or partially exempt from local real and personal property taxes. The Virginia Waste Minimization Program, a nonregulatory technical assistance program of the Virginia Department of Waste Management, provides information on reducing the volume and toxicity of the waste they produce to Virginia firms, local governments and other waste generators.

WASHINGTON

State of Washington, Department of Revenue
Olympia, Washington 98504-0090 (206) 753-5540

State of Washington, Department of Ecology
Mail Stop PV-11, Olympia, Washington 98504-8711 (206) 459-6000

Waste Reduction, Recycling and Litter Control Program
Department of Ecology, Olympia, Washington 98504 (206) 438-7541

Washington provides technical assistance and support to businesses from many offices of the Department of Ecology. In 1975 Washington established its 1-800-RECYCLE Information Hotline, thought to be the first in the country. The hotline received more than 250,000 calls during its first decade of operation, and has surpassed 10,000 calls in one month. The Waste Reduction, Recycling and Litter Control Program also provides technical assistance to businesses, including workshops on waste reduction and recycling targeted to specific types of businesses, site visits and industry-specific fact sheets.

WEST VIRGINIA

Department of Natural Resources Conservation, Education & Litter Control
1900 Washington Street East, Charleston, West Virginia 25305 (304) 348-3370

Department of Commerce, Labor and Environmental Resources
Office of the Secretary, State Capitol
Charleston, West Virginia 25305 (304) 348-3255

WISCONSIN

Wisconsin Department of Natural Resources
Box 7921 (SW/3), Madison, Wisconsin 53707 (608) 267-3763

State of Wisconsin, Department of Revenue
125 South Webster Street, P.O. Box 8933
Madison, Wisconsin 53708-8933 (608) 266-6466

Facilities for the treatment of industrial wastes or air contaminants are exempt from property taxes. Sales of tangible personal property becoming component parts of waste treatment facilities qualifying for that exemption are also exempt from the sales tax. Sales of waste reduction or recycling machinery and equipment, including parts for that equipment, are exempt when the property is used exclusively and directly for waste reduction or recycling. Effective for tax years ending after April 1, 1991, a recycling surcharge is imposed on all active corporations, sole proprietorships and partnerships.

WYOMING

Solid Waste Management Program
Wyoming Department of Environmental Quality
122 West 25th Street, Herschler Building
Cheyenne, Wyoming 82002 (307) 777-7752

The Council of State Governments
Iron Works Pike, P.O. Box 11910
Lexington, Kentucky 40578-1910 (800) 800-1910

This group publishes the Resource Guide to State Environmental management, a directory that lists more than 3,800 State Environmental contacts and environmental programs in each state.

Chapter 10

Helpful Resources For Your Business

The "green" movement is evident everywhere. Information on how we can change our habits and lifestyles to improve, preserve and protect our environment can be found in numerous magazines, books, talk shows, school curriculums, marketing campaigns and government publications.

Most of the available information is geared toward consumers, although some of it also may be helpful for businesses. Included in this chapter are listings of sources, other than federal and state governmental agencies, that may provide information, technical assistance or referrals that are better suited to the needs of businesses and small companies. Trade associations also may serve as a source for information or provide direction to suppliers, technicians or government contacts that may be helpful.

A major portion of the list is divided according to the chapters in this book, followed by resources that did not necessarily belong in any one chapter section. The list is by no means inclusive of all that might be available, but these resources can help you get started on your way to saving the earth.

RECYCLING

Aluminum Association
900 19th Street NW Suite 300, Washington, D.C. 20006 (202) 862-5100

Anchorage Recycling Center
6161 Rosewood, Anchorage, Alaska 99518 (907) 562-2267

Arizona Clean and Beautiful, Inc.
4350 East Camelback Road, Suite F100, Phoenix, Arizona 85018 (602) 840-3083

Arizona Recycling Hotline
2701 East Osborn Road, Suite 1, Phoenix, Arizona 85016 (602) 224-0836
(602) CLEAN-UP (800) 94-REUSE

Associated Recyclers of Montana
58 Charles Billings, Montana 59101 (406) 252-5721

Association of New Jersey Recyclers
120 Finderne Avenue, Bridgewater, New Jersey 08807 (201) 722-7575

Association of Oregon Recyclers
P.O. Box 15279, Portland, Oregon 97215 (503) 233-7770

Association of Vermont Recyclers
P.O. Box 1244, Montpelier, Vermont 05601 (802) 229-1833

California Resource Recovery Association
13223 Black Mountain Road Box 1-300, San Diego, California 92129
(619) 694-2161

Can Manufacturers Institute
1625 Massachusetts Avenue NW, Washington, D.C. 20036 (202) 232-4677

Colorado Recycles
1873 South Bellaire Street #510, Denver, Colorado 80222 (303) 691-5564

Connecticut Recyclers Coalition
P.O. Box 445, Stonington, Connecticut 06378 (203) 887-6368

Council of Plastics and Packaging in the Environment
1275 K Street NW Suite 900, Washington, D.C. 20005 (202) 789-1310

DC Department of Public Works Office of Recycling
65 K Street NE, Washington, D.C. 20003 (202) 727-5856

Delaware Solid Waste Authority
P.O. Box 455, Dover, Delaware 19903-0455 (302) 739-5365

EnviroSouth
P.O. Box 11468, Montgomery, Alabama 36111 (205) 277-7050

Exxon Oil Recycling Program, Exxon Company USA
800 Bell, Houston, Texas 77002 800-732-1100

Florida BIRP
7200-C Aloma Avenue, Winter Park, Florida 32792 (407) 678-4200

Georgia Department of Community Affairs, Georgia Clean and Beautiful
100 Peachtree Street NE, Atlanta, Georgia 30303 (404) 656-5534

Glass Packaging Institute
1801 K Street NW Suite 1105-L, Washington, D.C. 20006 (202) 887-4850

Illinois Association of Recycling Centers
P.O. Box 778, Park Ridge, Illinois 60068 (708) 825-5000

Indiana Recycling Coalition
P.O. Box 6357, Lafayette, Indiana 46903 (317) 283-6226

Institute of Scrap Recycling Industries
1627 K Street NW, Washington, D.C. 20006 (202) 466-4050

Iowa Recycling Association
P.O. Box 3184, Des Moines, Iowa 50316 (515) 265-4275

Kansas BIRP
2231 SW Wanamaker Road Suite 200, Topeka, Kansas 66614 (913) 273-6808

Keep MT Clean and Beautiful, Inc.
P.O. Box 5925, Helena, Montana 50604 (406) 443-6242

Kentucky BIRP
P.O. Box 1143, Frankfort, Kentucky 40602 (502) 227-7481

Kentucky Recycling Association, Urban County Government DPW
200 East Madison, Lexington, Kentucky 40507 (606) 258-3400

Maryland BIRP
584 Bellerive Drive Suite 3D, Annapolis, Maryland 21401 (301) 974-4472

MassRecycle
P.O. Box 3111, Worchester, Massachusetts 01613

Michigan Recycling Coalition
P.O. Box 10240, Lansing, Michigan 48901 (313) 849-2864

Missouri BIRP
P.O. Box 1336, Jefferson City, Missouri 65102 (314) 634-2725

NC Recycling Association
4505 Fair Meadow #210, Raleigh, North Carolina 27607 (919) 782-8933

NH Resource Recovery
P.O. Box 721, Concord, New Hampshire 03301-0721 (603) 224-6996

National Association for Plastic Container Recovery
5024 Parkway Plaza Boulevard, Charlotte, North Carolina 28217 (301) 565-0333

National Recycling Coalition
1101 30th Street NW, Washington, D.C. 20007 (202) 625-6406

National Soft Drink Association
1101 Sixteenth Street NW, Washington, D.C. 20036 (202)463-6732

Nebraska State Recycling Association
P.O. Box 80729, Lincoln, Nebraska 68501 (402) 475-3637

Official Recycled Products Guide
P.O. Box 577, Ogdensburg, New York 13669 (800) 267-0707

Ohio Industry Recycling Program
6057 Ashley Ct., Cincinnati, Ohio 45442 (513) 793-7409

Oklahoma BIRP
1000 North Mission, Sapulpa, Oklahoma 74066 (918) 227-1412

Pennsylvania Resources Council, Inc.
P.O. Box 88, Media, Pennsylvania 19063 (215) 565-9131

Recycle Minnesota Resources
1711 West County Road B, Suite 300N, Roseville, Minnesota 55113
(612) 635-0805

Recycle New Mexico
P.O. Box 27682, Albuquerque, New Mexico 87125 (505) 843-6400

Recycler's Trade Network (RTN)
800-786-1112

Recycling Association of Hawaii
162-B North King Street , Honolulu, Hawaii 96817 (808) 599-1976

Recycling Coalition of Texas
P.O. Box 2359, Austin, Texas 78768 (512) 458-7271

South Carolina Recycling Association
City of Aiken DPW, P.O. Box 1177, Aiken, South Carolina 29801 (803) 642-7610

Steel Can Recycling Institute
Foster Plaza 10, 680 Anderson Drive, Pittsburgh, Pennsylvania 15220
(412) 922-2772, (800) 867-7274

Tennessee Recycling Coalition
1010 18th Avenue South, Nashville, Tennessee 37212 (615) 329-0230

WI Serving our Environment (WISE)
606 East Wisconsin Avenue, Milwaukee, Wisconsin 53202 (414) 223-7520

Washington State Recycling Association
203 East 4th Avenue #307, Olympia, Washington 98501 (206) 352-8737
Hotlines: 800-Recycle and 800-Litter

West Virginia BIRP
P.O. Box 6508, Stonewall Station, Charleston, West Virginia 25062
(403) 344-0672

CONSERVATION

Air Conditioning Contractors of America
1513 16th Street NW, Washington, D. C. 20036 (202) 483-9370

Alliance to Save Energy
1725 K Street, NW, Washington, D.C. 20006-1401 (202) 857-0666

Alternative Sources of Energy
107 South Central Avenue, Milaca, Minnesota 56353 (612) 983-6892

American Council for an Energy-Efficient Economy
1001 Connecticut Avenue NW, Washington, D.C. 20036 (202) 624-2465

American Gas Association
1515 Wilson Boulevard, Arlington, Virginia 22209 (703) 841-8400

American Society of Heating, Refrigeration, and Air Conditioning Engineers
1791 Tullie Circle NE, Altanta, Georgia 30329 (404) 636-8400

American Solar Energy Society
2400 Central Ave., B-1, Boulder, Colorado 80301 (303) 443-3130

American Wind Energy Association
1730 North Lynn Street, Arlington, Virginia 22209 (703) 276-8334

Council on Alternative Fuels
1225 I Street NW, Ste. 320, Washington, D.C. 20005 (202)898-0711

Ecological Society of America
Arizona State University, Center for Environmental Studies, Tempe, AZ 85287
(602) 956-3000

Energy Conservation Coalition
1525 New Hampshire Avenue NW, Washington, D.C. 20036 (202) 745-4874

National Association of Environmental Professionals
P.O . Box 15210, Alexandria, Virginia 22309-0210 (703)660-3264

Northeast Utilities Conservation and Load Management Department
Dept ECC, P.O. Box 270, Hartford, Connecticut 06141 (203) 655-5000

Passive Solar Industries Council
1090 Vermont Ave. NW, Ste. 1200, Washington, D.C. 20005-4905 (202) 371-0357

Rocky Mountain Institute
1739 Snowmass Creek Road, Drawer 248, Snowmass, Colorado 81654-9199
(303) 927-3851

Solar Energy Industries Association
777 North Capitol Street, Suite 805, Washington, D.C. 20002 (202) 408-0660

POLLUTION AND TOXIN ELIMINATION

Acid Rain Foundation
1410 Varsity Drive, Raleigh, North Carolina 27606 (919) 828-9443

Air and Waste Management Association
P.O. Box 2861, Pittsburgh, Pennsylvania 15230 (412) 232-3444

American Association for Aerosol Research
5530 Wisconson Ave., Ste. 1149, Washington, D.C. 20815 (301) 907-9873

Association of American Pesticide Control Officials
Office of the Secretary, RR1 Box 1260, Greensboro, Vermont 05841
(802) 533-7704

Association for Commuter Transportation
808 17th St. NW, Suite 200, Washington, D.C. 20006 (202) 223-9669

Association of Local Air Pollution Control Officials
444 N Capitol Street NW, Ste. 306, Washington, D.C. 20001 (202) 624-7864

Manufacturers of Emission Controls Association
1707 L Street NW, Ste. 570, Washington, D.C 20036 (202) 296-4797

National Aeronautics and Space Administration
Building 2423, Stennis Space Center, Mississippi 39529

National Clean Air Coalition
801 Pennsylvania Avenue SE, Washington, D.C. 20003 (202) 543-8200

National Coalition Against Misuse of Pesticides
530 7th Street SE, Washington, D.C. 20003 (202) 543-5450.

National Council of the Paper Industry for Air and Stream Improvement
260 Madison Ave., New York, New York 10016 (212) 532-9000

National Toxics Campaign
P.O. Box 28171, Washington, D.C. 20005 (202) 291-0863.

Water and Wastewater Equipment Manufacturers Association
PO Box 17402, Dulles International Airport, Washington, D.C. 20041
(703) 444-1777

Water Pollution Control Federation
601 Wythe Street, Lexandria, Vermont 22314-1994

ENVIRONMENTALLY SAFE PRODUCTS

Green Cross
1611 Telegraph Ave., Ste 1111, Oakland, California 94612.

Green Seal
P.O. Box 1694, Palo Alto, CA 94302.

WASTE MANAGEMENT

Citizen's Clearinghouse For Hazardous Wastes, Inc.
P.O. Box 926, Arlington, Virginia 22216 (703) 276-7070

Council for Solid Waste Solutions
1275 K Street NW, Washington, D.C. 20005 (202) 371-5319

Direct Marketing Association
6 East 43rd Street, New York, New York 10017 (212) 768-7277

Environmental Hazards Management Institute
10 Newmarket Road, Durham, New Hampshire 03824 (603) 868-1496

Great Lakes/Midwest Waste Exchange
400 Ann Street SW Suite 201A, Grand Rapids, Michigan 49504-2054
(616) 363-3262

Hazardous Materials Control Research Institute
7237 Hanover Parkway, Greenbelt, Maryland 20770 (301) 587-9390

Industrial Material Exchange Service
2200 Churchill Road #24, Springfield, Illinois 62794-0276 (217) 782-0450

National Solid Waste Management Association, Waste Recyclers Council
1730 Rhode Island Avenue NW, Suite 1000 , Washington, D.C. 20036
(202) 659-4613.

Northeast Industrial Waste Exchange
90 Presidential Plaza, Suite 122, Syracuse, New York 13202 (315) 422-6572

Resource Management Associates, Inc.
P.O. Box 251, West Barnstable, Massachusetts 02688

Solid Waste Resource Center, American Paper Institute
1250 Connecticut Avenue NW, Washington, D.C. (800) 878-8878

Southeast Waste Exchange, Urban Institute,Department of Civil Engineering
University of North Carolina at Charlotte, Charlotte, North Carolina 28223
(704) 547-2307

Southern Waste Information Exchange
P.O. Box 960, Tallahassee, Florida 32302 (800) 441-SWIX

Waste Management, Inc.
3003 Butterfield Road, Oak Brook, Illinois 60521

Waste and WasteWater Equipment Manufacturing Association
101 East Holly Avenue Suite 14, Sterling, Virginia 22170 (703) 444-1777

PRESERVATION OF RESOURCES AND WILDLIFE

American Forest Council
1250 Connecticut Avenue NW, Washington, D.C. 20036 (202) 463-2455

American Forestry Association Global ReLeaf
P.O. Box 2000, Washington, D.C. 20013 (202) 667-3300

American Rivers, Inc.
801 Pennsylvania Avenue SE, Suite 303, Washington, D.C. 20003
(202) 547-6900

American Water Resources Association
5410 Grosvenor Lane, Bethesda, Maryland 20814 (301) 794-7711

Association for Conservation Information
P.O. Box 10678, Reno, Nevada 89520 (702) 688-1500

Center for Marine Conservation
1725 DeSales StreetNW, Suite 500, Washington, D.C. 20036 (202) 429-5609

Clean Water Action Project
317 Pennsylvania Avenue SE, Washington, D.C. 20003 (202) 547-1196

Conservation Foundation/World Wildlife Fund
1250 24th Street NW, Washington, D.C. 20037 (202) 293-4800

National Audubon Society
950 Third Avenue, New York, New York 10022 (212) 832-3200

National Wildlife Federation
1400 16th Street NW, Washington, D.C. 20036-2266 (800)-432-6564

Natural Resources Defense Council
40 West 20th Street, New York, New York 10011 (212) 727-2700

Nature Conservancy
1815 North Lynn Street, Arlington, Virginia 22209 (703) 841-5300

Rainforest Action Network
301 Broadway, Suite A, San Francisco, California 94133 (415) 398-4404

Rainforest Alliance
270 Layfayette Street, Suite 512, New York, New York 10012 (212) 941-1900

Renewable Natural Resources Foundation
5430 Grosvenor Ln., Bethesda, Maryland 20814 (301) 493-9101

Sierra Club
730 Polk Street, San Francisco, California 94109 (415) 776-2211

Trees for the Future
11306 Estona Drive, P.O. Box 1786, Silver Spring, Maryland 20915

Water Information Network
P.O. Box 909, Ashland, Oregon 97520 (800)-533-6714

Wilderness Society
1400 I Street NW, Suite 550, Washington, D.C. 20205 (202) 842-3400

Wildlife Habitat Enhancement Council
1010 Wayne Avenue, Suite 1240, Silver Spring, Maryland 20910 (301) 588-8994

SPECIAL MEASURES

EcoExpos
9348 Civic Center Drive, Beverly Hills, CA 90210 (213) 278-1460

Environmental Communication Associates
1881 9th Street Boulder, Colorado 80302 (303) 444-1428

ENVIRONMENT/GENERAL

Council on Economic Priorities
30 Irving Place, New York, New York 10003 (212) 420-1133

Council on Environmental Quality
722 Jackson Place NW, Washington, D.C. 20006 (202) 395-5750

Earth Action Network
28 Knight Street, Norwalk, Connecticut 06851 (203) 854-5559

Environmental Action Foundation
1525 New Hamprshire Avenue NW, Washington, D.C. 20036 (202) 745-4879

Environmental Defense Fund
257 Park Avenue South, New York, New York 10010 (212) 505-2100

Green Business Letter
1526 Connecticut Avenue NW, Washington, D.C. 20036 (800) 955- GREEN

Greenpeace
1436 U Street NW, Washington, D.C. 20009 (202) 462-1177 / 462-8817

Keep America Beautiful
Mill River Plaza, 9 West Broad Street, Stamford, Connecticut 06902
(203) 323-8987

World Resources Institute
1709 New York Avenue NW, Suite 700, Washington, D.C. 20006 (202) 638-6300

The Greenpeace Guide to Paper, Greenpeace Northwest
4649 Sunnyside Avenue North, Seattle, Washington 98103

Chapter 11

Awards & Recognition For Saving The Earth

The motives behind the actions of business owners to save the earth are as varied as their companies. A positive impact on the bottom line is one of the most compelling reasons to preserve resources, prevent pollution and waste, recycle and conserve energy. Other reasons also weigh into the decision to initiate or continue business practices that are considerate of the environment. Capturing market share or enhancing product positioning; gaining community goodwill and a positive public image; or providing consumer education and educating children about the environment are some of the other reasons for companies to make environmental efforts.

Another important reason is recognition. Everyone likes to be recognized for their hard work and successes. Business owners and managers are no different. Regardless of their motives, businessmen and businesswomen appreciate recognition for their efforts and the positive publicity it brings. Recognition is something Ramada International Hotels & Resorts reaped for its efforts. The case study that follows shows how Ramada was able to gain international recognition for its environmental efforts.

Ramada International Wins Industry Environmental Award

Ramada International Hotels & Resorts was named winner of the 1991 International Hotel Association (IHA) Environmental Award during ceremonies in Sweden. This prestigious award, cosponsored by the IHA and American Express, is based upon energy-saving benefits, creativity of the program, involvement of staff and management in project implementation and communication of benefits to hotel guests.

"The winning entry was thoroughly comprehensive in its approach to energy conservation, involving every member of the hotel staff in addition to top management and the hotel guest," said Helge Holgersen, IHA president.

In April 1990, Phoenix-based Ramada International President and CEO Bill Grau launched an environmental program that challenged 28,000 employees worldwide to initiate changes that would recycle waste at more than 100 hotels in 36 countries. During the first year, the program was very much a "grass-roots" effort with hundreds of ideas coming from every area of hotel operation.

Items recycled range from aluminum cans to cooking grease and oil. Paper is a primary target of the program: guest room directories, all menus (including those hung on guestroom doors), telephone notepads, guest checks and folios. Recycling is complemented by extensive replacement: styrofoam cups are replaced with glassware, paper napkins with linen napkins, and carryout styrofoam boxes with paper bags.

As a result of their efforts, Ramada also has won other awards. Ramada's environmental program was a finalist in *Travel and Leisure* magazine's "Mark of Innovation Awards" for 1990 and it was one of three U.S. corporations featured by *Incentive Magazine* in January 1991 for employee involvement in its environmental program.

Awards and recognition have not been confined to just the corporate office. In May 1991, the Ramada Renaissance Hotel Atlanta-Airport received the industry's highest honor for Environmental Quality Achievement from the American Hotel and Motel Association (AH&MA). The individual hotel was cited for improvement of the environmental quality in terms of property/community beautification, natural resources, and conservation.

The 469-room airport hotel implemented an "Adopt-A-Street" program where hotel employees gathered weekly to collect trash along a one-mile stretch of highway near the hotel. Daily efforts include recycling of cooking grease and oil, white paper, glass and aluminum cans. As a result of these combined efforts, they estimate 1,100 trees were saved and the hotel's energy consumption was reduced by 9 percent.

Award Programs

Many special award and recognition programs have been developed by industry, government and environmental associations. These programs not only honor businesses for their exemplary role in environmental protection, but also provide examples and set standards for other companies to follow. Many awards programs can be found by contacting your local federal, state and municipal government agencies, or industrial and environmental associations.

An alphabetical listing of many of the groups that bestow awards and a brief description of their awards that may be applicable to business follows.

Listing Of Awards And Award Programs

AMERICAN ASSOCIATION OF NURSERYMEN
1250 I Street NW, Suite 500, Washington, D.C. 20005 (202) 789-2900

American Beautification Award Awarded for outstanding contributions to environmental improvement by use of living plants.

Green Survival City Award This award honors business and community leaders for their role in improvements in their cities.

National Landscape Award Given to businesses, institutions, and government agencies that save the earth through use of landscaping and have made a significant contribution to the quality of life in their community.

AMERICAN FORESTRY ASSOCIATION
1516 P Street NW Washington, D.C. 20005 (202) 667-3300

National Tree Planting Award Given to an individual or organization for significant program in reforestation.

AMERICAN PAPER INSTITUTE
260 Madison Avenue, New York, New York 10016 (212) 340-0600

Environmental and Energy Achievement Awards Program Recognizes paper industry and forest products companies for their outstanding achievements in improving the environment.

ASSOCIATION OF CONSERVATION ENGINEERS
Alabama Department of Conservation,
64 North Union Street, Montgomery, Alabama 36130 (202) 261-3476

Eugene Baker Memorial Award Recognizes an engineer for contributions to conservation engineering.

CHEVRON, USA
Corporate Program Director, P.O. Box 7753, San Francisco, California 94120-7753 (415) 894-2457

Chevron Conservation Awards This program honors individuals and organizations for their outstanding contribution regarding the conservation of natural resources.

CONNECTICUT RIVER WATERSHED COUNCIL
125 Combs Road E., Hampton, Massachusetts 01027 (413) 584-0057

Certificate of Conservation Awards Honors distinguished service by the media, organizations, individuals, and corporations in their conservation efforts in the Connecticut River Valley.

COUNCIL ON ECONOMIC PRIORITIES
30 Irving Place, ATN: CCA-92, New York, New York 10003 (212) 420-1133

The Council on Economic Priorities "Corporate Conscience Awards" program Honors companies for their innovative, unique or long-standing programs in the areas of community action, equal opportunity, responsiveness to employees, charitable giving, and environmental stewardship.

ECOLOGICAL SOCIETY OF AMERICA
Center for Environmental Services, Arizona State University,
Tempe, Arizona 85287 (602) 965-3000

This corporate award is given to recognize businesses for their accomplishments in integrating environmentally conscious concepts into their procedures.

ENVIRONMENTAL INDUSTRY COUNCIL
1825 K Street NW, Suite 210 Washington, D.C. 20006 (202) 331-7706

National Environmental Industry Awards Given to provide recognition to companies for their outstanding technological achievements and leadership in five environmental categories.

FLORIDA AUDUBON SOCIETY
1101 Audubon Way Maitland, Florida 32751 (407) 647-2615

Corporate Award Given to honor industry for outstanding contributions to environmental issues.

GLOBAL TOMORROW COALITION
1325 G Street NW, Suite 915, Washington, D.C. 20005-3014 (2020) 628-4016

Lorax Award Given to recognize leadership in bringing environmental concerns and issues to the attention of the public.

KEEP AMERICA BEAUTIFUL
Mill River Plaza, 9 West Broad Street, Stamford, Connecticut 06902
(203) 3232-8987

Several awards offered by this organization may be appropriate for businesses.

MINNESOTA GOVERNOR'S AWARDS FOR EXCELLENCE
IN POLLUTION PREVENTION
Minnesota Office of Waste Management, 1350 Energy Lane, St. Paul, Minnesota 55108 (612) 649-5750 Toll free in Minnesota 1-800-652-9747

This annual program honors Minnesota businesses, institutions, organizations and individuals for their creative approaches to pollution prevention at the source.

NATIONAL ASSOCIATION OF CONSERVATION DISTRICTS
509 Capitol Court NE, Washington, D.C. 20005 (202) 547-6223

Business Conservation Leadership Award Given to honor a local business, corporation or corporate division that has implemented outstanding resource management practices on their property with cooperation of a local conservation district.

NATIONAL ASSOCIATION FOR ENVIRONMENTAL EDUCATION
P.O. BOX 400, Troy, Ohio 45373 (513) 698-6493

Annual award to organizations and individuals for outstanding service in the field of environmental education.

NATIONAL ENERGY RESOURCES ORGANIZATION
The Flanagan Group 11 Canal Center, Station 250 Alexandria, Virginia 22314
(703) 739-8822

Energy Conservation Award Given to a person, organization, or group that was responsible for an unusual activity related to energy conservation.

NATIONAL RECYCLING COALITION
P.O. Box 80729, Lincoln, Nebraska 68501 (402) 475-3637

Outstanding Innovation Award Given to recognize companies for their notable achievements in recycling.

Outstanding Program Awards For outstanding recycling programs. Categories include curbside recycling, buyback recycling, volunteer recycling, regional recycling, recycling industry and business recycling.

NATIONAL WILDLIFE FEDERATION
c/o Corporate Conservation Council, 1400 16th Street NW, Washington, D.C.
20036-2266 (202) 797-6800

*Environmental Achievement Award Given to honor an American business that has
developed a conservation project that sets an outstanding example.*

*National Conservation Achievement Awards Program To honor those
achievements that deserve national recognition. Corporate leadership is one of the
categories in this program.*

NEW YORK BOTANICAL GARDEN
c/o Education Department Southern Boulevard and East 200th Street
Bronx, New York 10458 (212) 220-8700

*Green World Award Given to honor businesses, corporation, individuals, scientists
or leading public figures for their significant achievement in environmental
conservation.*

POWER
McGraw-Hill, Inc. 11 West 19th Street, New York, New York 10011
(212) 337-4060

*Energy Conservation Award To recognize industry for the steps taken to conserve
energy.*

*Environmental Protection Award Recognizes power plants for their outstanding
efforts to improve environmental quality.*

PRESIDENT'S ENVIRONMENT AND CONSERVATION CHALLENGE
AWARDS

*This program is administered by the Council on Environmental Quality in a
partnership with The National Geographic Society, The Hearst Corporation, The
Business Roundtable, and the World Wildlife fund. Nine awards and 23 citations were
in 1991, the first year of the awards.*

PROFESSIONAL BUILDER
1350 East Touhy Avenue, Des Plaines, Illinois 60018

*Best In American Living Awards To recognize successful new housing designs for
outstanding design, construction, and energy efficiency.*

RENEW AMERICA
1400 16th Street NW, Suite 710, Washington, D.C. 20036 (202) 232-2252

*National Environmental Achievement Award - Searching for Success Program
Awards in 21 categories to recognize successful environmental programs in existence
for at least six months.*

SIERRA CLUB
Board of Director's Coordinator, 730 Polk Street, San Francisco, California
94109 (415) 776-22211

*Earthcare Award Given to recognize an organization, agency or individual for a
unique contribution to international environmental protection and conservation.*

SOIL AND WATER CONSERVATION SOCIETY
7515 NE Ankeny Road, Ankeny, Iowa 50021-9764 (515) 289-2331

Merit Award Given for outstanding effort or activity promoting wise land use. Recipients can be a corporation, business, or organization.

UNITED STATES ARMY CORPS OF ENGINEERS
20 Massachusetts Avenue NW, Washington, D.C. 20314 (202) 272-0011

Chief of Engineers Design and Environmental Awards Program Civil works and military construction projects are eligible.

UNIVERSITY OF SOUTHERN CALIFORNIA
John and Alice Tyler Ecology/Energy Prize Provost's, Office University of Southern California, Los Angeles, California 90089-4019 (213) 743-6343

Tyler Prize for Environmental Achievement Given to individuals, corporations or other institutions that have made a significant contribution in the environmental field.

VALLEY FORWARD ASSOCIATION
4350 East Camelback Road, Suite 200C, Phoenix, Arizona 85018 (602) 952-1300

Valley Forward Association, a nonprofit public interest group dedicated to promoting the aesthetic, cultural and environmental interests in the metropolitan Phoenix area, presents its "Crescordia" Environmental Excellence Awards annually.

WILDLIFE SOCIETY
5410 Grosvenor Lane Bethesda, Maryland 20814 (301) 897-9770

Group Achievement Award Given to honor an organization for outstanding wildlife achievement.

WORLD ENVIRONMENT CENTER
419 Park Avenue South, Suite 1403 New York, New York 10016 (212) 683-4700

Gold Medal Award for International Corporate Environmental Achievement To honor a corporation for its outstanding and well-implemented environmental policy. Corporations with substantial international operations are considered.

WORLD WILDLIFE FUND
1250 24th Street NW, Washington, D.C. 20037 (202) 778-9555

J. Paul Getty Wildlife Conservation Prize Individuals and organizations are selected for their direct or indirect international impact on wildlife conservation.

Certificate of Merit Given to department stores and furriers in the US who have pledged not to buy or sell skins of finished products of wild animals on the endangered species list prepared by the World Wildlife Fund.

Chapter 12

Getting Started

Saving the earth is a monumental task. It will take the consistent, dedicated and effective international efforts of concerned citizens and individuals in business, industry, education and government.

The many companies included in this book are just a sampling of those already working to make saving the earth part of their every day operations and long-range planning. They have realized it is good for the earth, and also good for their businesses.

Consumers are demanding environmentally sensitive products. More frequently, they are making their purchasing decisions based not only upon the product itself, but on the company's record on environmental issues and company practices.

Can your business meet your customers' expectations, make a contribution to saving the earth, and still make a profit? Yes it can! Here are some forms, instructions and worksheets to help you set up a simple plan so you can get started saving the earth.

10-STEP ENVIRONMENTAL ACTION PLAN

Step 1

Assign one person or a small committee the responsibility of developing and implementing an environmental plan for your business. Remember, changing the ways you have been doing things, and getting people to change how they think about saving the earth at work isn't going to happen overnight. It will take a deliberate, well planned effort managed by a responsible and respected member of your staff.

Step 2

Conduct an environmental audit of your business to determine what opportunities exist at your business to save the earth. Prioritize those areas in terms of cost-effectiveness and benefit to the environment as well as to your business.

Step 3

Select one environmental area at a time, whether it's recycling, pollution control or waste management. It is too difficult to try and tackle several things at once.

Step 4

Set your goal. Develop a plan and a realistic time frame for what you want to accomplish. Do you want to recycle only paper? Aluminum cans? Glass? Newspapers? Are you looking for a way to conserve energy in your business? How about decreasing landfill tipping fees by better waste management?

Step 5

Contact government or other resources for technical assistance. Expertise and some grant money often is available at no cost to your business.

Step 6

Communicate and promote the plan to all your employees. Get them involved. They may have some great ideas on how to accomplish the goal, and have fun at the same time.

Step 7

Implement your plan and continue to monitor the results. The best plan in the world isn't going to work if it isn't managed effectively.

Step 8

Celebrate your accomplishments. Let your employees know how much you appreciate their efforts in helping your company save the earth and save money. Reward your employees' good ideas with Save The Earth mugs and t-shirts.

Step 9

Publicize your results. Let your customers and your community know what you are doing. Perhaps you can incorporate information about what you are doing into your marketing plan or advertising. Contact your local print and broadcast news media to let them know about your successes.

Step 10

Select another area of opportunity for your business to save the earth. Repeat these steps to incorporate it into your environmental action plan and daily business operations.

ENVIRONMENTAL AUDIT

Date: _____

Review all the areas of your business and list possible
opportunities to save the earth in each of these areas.
Review the How To's provided at the end of each chapter
and list those that might work for your business. Add other
considerations you or your staff discover.

RECYCLING:

_____

_____

_____

_____

CONSERVATION:

_____

_____

_____

_____

POLLUTION AND TOXIN ELIMINATION:

_____

_____

_____

_____

ENVIRONMENTALLY SAFE PRODUCTS & SERVICES:
(for development or for use in your business)

_____

_____

_____

_____

WASTE MANAGEMENT:

_____

_____

_____

_____

PRESERVATION OF NATURAL RESOURCES & WILDLIFE:

_____

_____

_____

_____

SPECIAL MEASURES OR PROMOTIONAL IDEAS:

_____

_____

_____

_____

ENVIRONMENTAL ACTION REVIEW

Review the opportunities you have identified in your environmental audit. Prioritize each according to the potential benefit to your business and the environment. Generate a form similar to the one that follows for each activity. Analyze your need for technical assistance and support to implement the action. Review chapters 10 and 11 for possible resources you might contact and list them on this form.

ENVIRONMENTAL ACTION PLANNER

Activity: _____

Desired Benefit to the Environment:

Desired Benefit to the Business:

Technical Assistance or Information Needed:

Responsible Person(s):_____

Start Date:_____ Target Completion Date:_____

Approximate Cost to Implement: $_____

Anticipated Dollar Savings: $_____

Technical Support Contact(s):

Major Steps in Implementing Plan:

Employee Involvement:

Ideas to Publicize Results or Achieve Recognition:

Index

Available From The Publisher

Special Editions and Quantity Discounts

SAVE MONEY & SAVE THE EARTH can be customized as a special edition for your business or organization. In addition, quantity discounts are available for businesses, groups and organizations who are interested in using the book as a promotional tool or fundraising vehicle.

Coffee Mugs & T-shirts, Too!

Attractive coffee mugs and T-shirts with the slogan, **SAVING THE EARTH IS GOOD BUSINESS**, also are available from the publisher. The mugs and T-shirts can be used with employee environmental suggestion programs, as customer appreciation gifts or with other promotional activities your business or organization can implement to make others aware of what your business is doing to save the earth. A FREE idea check list comes with every order.

Call or write for more information:

Marketing Methods Press
1413 E. Marshall Avenue
Phoenix, AZ 85014
1-(800)-745-5047
(602) 840-7308